"Jan Bowen's insight to overcome our fears and create a [...] is amazing. *It's Not That Complicated* makes it easy to c[...] that challenge you to look inside your hearts and you[...] Her wisdom helps you eliminate the negative, enabling you to 'Trust Forward.' Not complicated at all if you follow her direction, be honest, and take action. This book is a must read for those who know where they want to go but don't know how to get there."

—Susan Tidswell, president and founder, CRO-Inc.

"Having worked side by side with Jan, I know her message comes from her own purpose and mission. She lives and writes from a place of deep connection, truth, and realism! Read this book for practical yet powerful tools and create your own Personal Template for a successful and fulfilling life."

—Alan Seale, director, Center for Transformational Presence, author of *Create A World That Works* and *The Power of Your Presence*

"At the heart of Jan Bowen's success are incredible listening skills that enable her to intuit exactly what people are thinking and feeling. Those listening skills, coupled with a keenly analytical mind and uncommon empathy, make her a reliable observer of human behavior and a great coach. She has transferred this ability in her book and shows ways you can create a personalized Template of practical tools to keep yourself in alignment with your values and purpose."

—John A. Higgins, private equity communications and strategy advisor

"Whether you are in business or looking for your next step in life, this book can help you clarify where to go next and how to feel good about it. Jan shows that it really isn't that complicated to set up a routine that supports how you most want to work and live."

—Ian Gover, cofounder, Everwise

IT'S NOT THAT

complicated

JAN L. BOWEN

IT'S NOT THAT

complicated

How to Create a Personalized
Template of Alignment

Published by Advantage, Charleston, South Carolina.
Member of Advantage Media Group.

ADVANTAGE is a registered trademark and the Advantage colophon is a trademark of Advantage Media Group, Inc.

Printed in the United States of America.

ISBN: 978-1-59932-658-0
LCCN: 2015955117

Book design by Megan Elger.

This publication is designed to provide accurate and authoritative information in regard to the subject matter covered. It is sold with the understanding that the publisher is not engaged in rendering legal, accounting, or other professional services. If legal advice or other expert assistance is required, the services of a competent professional person should be sought.

Some names and identifying details have been changed to protect the privacy of individuals.

Advantage Media Group is proud to be a part of the Tree Neutral® program. Tree Neutral offsets the number of trees consumed in the production and printing of this book by taking proactive steps such as planting trees in direct proportion to the number of trees used to print books. To learn more about Tree Neutral, please visit www.treeneutral.com. To learn more about Advantage's commitment to being a responsible steward of the environment, please visit www.advantagefamily.com/green

To Mom & Dad, from the beginning.

To George, always & forever.

Contents

Acknowledgments

I have been blessed with lifelong support. Expressing my appreciation for the individuals who have had a part in making this book and my work a reality would fill a book in itself. While it would be impossible to name everyone to whom I am grateful, the following is a short list.

To George, for sharing life with me—I couldn't be luckier or happier. Thank you. To my companions from birth and those who joined along the way—Adelle and Ed and their families—deepest love to you all. To all my coworkers and clients, past and present, my appreciation is boundless. To Karen B, your support means more to me than you may ever realize. To my friends near and far, my gratitude for you has no boundary.

To Cris Gladly, my first editor—thank you for showing me what a pleasure sharing my writing could be. Working with you is an unreserved delight. To Scott Neville, working with you only reinforced my opinion that editors are a gift to writers—thank you for making the process fun and always having my back. To Patti, Megan, Brette, and "my" team at Advantage—deep thanks for the beautiful work you do that captures me so truly.

And to those many people along the way, thank you for calling out for this book. I hope I've answered your call.

Look To This Day

For it is life,

The very life of life.

In its brief course lie all

The realities and verities of existence,

The bliss of growth,

The splendor of action,

The glory of power —

For yesterday is but a dream,

And tomorrow is only a vision.

But today, well lived,

Makes every yesterday a dream of happiness

And every tomorrow a vision of hope.

Look well, therefore, to this day.

SANSKRIT PROVERB BY KALIDASA

Revealing a Full-Spectrum Life

One does not become enlightened by imagining figures
of light but by making the darkness conscious.

—CARL JUNG

Life isn't that complicated. Nature has an inherent order and balance, but we confuse things and then spend many hours searching to simplify and figure everything out.

It is through aligning our whole being—our talents, skills, values, purpose, energy, and style—with our external world that allows us to simplify life and find peace of mind and joy. Take a moment and imagine your spine straightening, shoulders pulling back, chin lifting, and head raising. That image suggests someone who is inspired to take control and move forward with focus.

For the purpose of this book, complete alignment is attained when you find your unique, personal journey in the world and are able to maintain your place in it. Much like a fingerprint, your personal zone should feel like part of you. When you are acting and moving with alignment, life feels effortless. Daily life and your part in it appear seamless. But how do we create that alignment? Is it something we are born with? Do we become misaligned over time?

These are the questions you will consider as you begin creating your Personal Template. You will consider the two following questions:

1. Can you clearly articulate your *values?*

2. What is your *purpose in life?*

To create permanent alignment within yourself requires total clarity on these two questions. You will begin to feel a growing sense of clarity as we explore these two questions in Part 1.

Once you have clearly identified your values and life purpose, Part 2 helps you to create a plan for personal alignment—an individualized strategy that specifically responds to your needs. This strategy, known as your Personal Template, is a comprehensive, three-part toolkit that we will be built on the following foundational components:

1. A Daily Practice

2. A Structure of Tactics

3. A Bundle of Exceptional Resources

There is a unifying thread of knowledge through everyone's purpose. This thread stretches across each facet of our lives and is strengthened as we learn more about ourselves and as we progress and grow from that knowledge. As we individually expand our information, we benefit from strengthening our capability to process all the various forms of input in our lives. This book shows you how to organize your process and establish your Daily Practice, Structure of Tactics, and Bundle of Exceptional Resources. Your Daily Practice serves to erase the day before and open a fresh slate by using routine actions you begin to rely on. The Structure of Tactics is a customized set of habits you form to respond to particular needs you have, to set yourself up for daily success and reinforce positive daily action. Exceptional Resources are a bundle of additional actions for when you need extra help during especially challenging times. By building all three of these components of your Personal Template, you will give yourself the tools to increase your potential and be in alignment.

Once you begin to value your purpose and the work that you do as part of that, you begin to see it as larger than yourself—accepting yourself as an individual with a unique purpose, bundled together with your specific gifts and imperfections, and joyfully bringing those forward.

No information is truly new. What appears new is the way in which we put it together. No one else has your answers. All the answers you need are within you. Any help you seek through a book, therapist, guide, or coach will only assist you in unlocking what is already within. Deciphering what is already in you and determining what is meaningful is ultimately up to you. My hope is that the way I have put this information together will help you create or clarify your own Personal Template and provide support as you go forward.

Your job is to polish the role you have with all the passion you possess and to fully participate in this life as only you can. Then, as you integrate your values with your purpose in the world, you enter full-spectrum living. You are able to align the physical, mental, and spiritual components of yourself while living in balance. That is the peace and joy that is available as you proceed on this expedition.

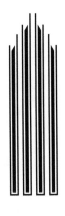

part one

THE GROUNDWORK

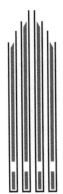

chapter one

Trust Forward: Make It Happen

The important thing is not to stop questioning. Curiosity has its own reason for existing. One cannot help but be in awe when he contemplates the mysteries of eternity, of life, of the marvelous structure of reality. It is enough if one tries merely to comprehend a little of this mystery every day. Never lose a holy curiosity.

—ALBERT EINSTEIN

Anytime you embark on a new project, it's customary to encounter a certain amount of resistance. You are asking yourself to invest a tremendous amount of trust in the unknown—in a new approach, a different way of thinking, and an altered way of being. You're requiring yourself to change the way you think and act.

This is no small matter. It is, in fact, the difference between the three options of living life: fully with joyful purpose, staying stuck, or going backward. When you choose to move toward your vision, I call that "trusting forward." Until you make that choice, you are unable to progress with your mission in life.

It is tremendously brave to routinely trust forward despite all odds. Many people take one stab at their dream and give up. To continue to endure the hardships with no light at the end of the tunnel is an act of faith. It takes digging deep into your values to believe you have what it takes to get to your objective. If your aspiration is significant enough to you and your purpose, you *will* have the necessary endurance.

Beliefs shape our behaviors–influencing how effectively we can progress based on our thoughts about success, goal obtainment, and our worthiness to live our dreams. We stretch our beliefs by trusting through reluctance, uncertainty, fear, and any other emotions that hold us back. In order to move forward with our plans, we have to overcome restrictive emotions, let go of the reins, and trust in the unpredictable outcome.

For those of us accustomed to being in charge and taking the lead to accomplish results, this can be difficult. But if we look at it another way, not taking the lead can be a relief from the pressure of having to take action and affect change. Not being the sole driver can be liberating.

It all starts with believing in yourself. By trusting forward, you are committing to believing in your abilities to push forward into an unpredictable future. This book walks you through the process of letting go of pieces of your life that hold you back while simultaneously discovering ways to move forward toward a more fulfilling existence.

Fear is a driving force in a lack of ability to trust forward. To completely push past the fear and trust yourself, you need to understand what you are really afraid of. In the large scheme of life, there are two overriding emotions at the opposite ends of the spectrum—love and fear. All other emotions derive in some way from these. You can translate them into alternative words for varying intensity of those emotions, but at the base is love and fear.

In the next few chapters, we explore your values, your life purpose, and a variety of life tools and skills to help you accomplish what you most want in life. Before we start, the following exercise will set up the expedition by reminding you of your favorite aspects of yourself. Before you ask yourself to trust forward, it is helpful to be able to fully enjoy who you are now.

The Exercises that follow are also available as a file for you to conveniently download and complete. To access, go to www.ItsNotThatComplicatedToolKit.com

EXERCISE ONE
MY FAVORITE QUALITIES[1]

As you create your Personal Template in this book, begin by asking yourself what you want to accomplish from this project. Set up a notebook, journal, or folder in the form of your choice—digital or paper—that will be your Book of Me for your Personal Template. Set it up to visually represent you or the future you. Take some quiet time for reflection and consider the following, making notes in your designated notebook:

1. Think of your ideal self. Take time to consider every aspect of your life. Make a list of 50-100 qualities that uniquely describe you. Include talents, traits, and characteristics of all facets of your life—work, home, hobbies, dreams, personality traits, and so on. Examples could include: passionate about African wildlife, witty, ride motorcycle, quick to judge others, compulsive list maker, need to have clean house, kind, impatient.

---

1 Exercise adapted from *The Coaching Tools Company*

Reread your list, and consider whether it describes you adequately. If a family member or best friend were to read that list, would they know you were being described? If not, prune and add until it suits you precisely.

2. Now, imagine you are traveling on a road that takes you to your envisioned, full-spectrum life. You encounter an omni-powerful presence who can grant all your wishes and dreams. But in order for those dreams to come true, you must give up 30 percent of your qualities. Look through your list and choose which qualities to sacrifice. Take some time to reflect on why you chose to sacrifice certain qualities.

3. You continue on this road, and again are told you must give up 30 percent of your qualities. Choose your second 30 percent. Reflect on why you chose those qualities. (Hint: you are traveling a road to your future self. You may want to keep the qualities that best represent that self.)

4. As you travel along, you are told once again to sacrifice 30 percent of your qualities, but this will be the last time. Observe which are your final choices to let go.

5. Now look at the list. These are the qualities you most appreciate about yourself. Reflect on these and what they mean to you.

6. Are you using your favorite qualities? If yes, are you using them often or to their full advantage? Why or why not?

7. How can you use your final list to empower you to push through your fears going forward?

BE REAL

Fear can be crippling and can often leave you directionless. Before you get determined to push past it, though, it's important to acknowledge the emotions you are feeling. Being in alignment means living in integrity—being consistent in words, thoughts, and actions. Pretending or hiding emotions can slowly result in misalignment and quite often backfires. Start by accepting whatever your emotions are and then handle them responsibly. Learn to coexist with fear or doubt or anger and move through it. That is the way that fear will back down and lose its power.

If you hide discouragement or hesitation, you are constructing a false persona and showing a face to the outside world that doesn't match the one within you. When your mask is on, you are blind and unable to see the greater potential in your life.

By acknowledging your emotions and taking control of your response to them, you are accepting your accountability as an adult. Accountability challenges us to be honest and to take responsibility for our reactions to the world around us. It takes courage to drop the mask and step forward with authenticity, but the action you take will be reinforced by increased motivation.

When you admit how you truly feel, you can approach your obstacle without getting stuck and exacerbating or extending the fear. The point isn't to deny the emotion of a situation. Rather, you realize the intensity of the experience and move through it with a new level of insight, understanding, and emotional intelligence. Seeing it in this way, you can begin to see options to transform situations. You begin to embody a new reality that incorporates the new lessons learned along with all that came before.

Once you take control by finding a solution, you will begin to build reassurance and self-confidence. Fear becomes a demarcation line for action, and the creativity used in generating potential responses erodes the fear and ramps up enthusiasm and encouragement. **Powerful alignment results when you are directed by and focused on your purpose.**

To get to the root of a fear, ask yourself what outcome you want. The answer will probably have something to do with living your purpose. When you are willing to take a risk and take action, you may find not only the dream you were looking for but also a far greater result: empowerment.

At our best, we are efficient machines. Our brains create structured patterns within neural pathways to organize information and allow optimal functioning. The brain works with whatever information it has. If negative thoughts or counterproductive behaviors are dominant in your life, your brain will organize those into a very orderly pattern so that you can function systematically with those thoughts and behaviors.[2] When you want to change your behavior to a more productive outcome, positive input needs to be substituted on which the brain can form new patterns. Be accountable by asking yourself what one step you *can* do. Break whatever pattern of behavior isn't working for you and begin creating one that will. The following exercise can help you make this transition.

---

2 Dr. Norman Doidge, *The Brain That Changes Itself: Stories of Personal Triumph from the Frontiers of Brain Science* (New York: Penguin, 2007).

EXERCISE TWO
BURN THROUGH THE DOUBT

In this exercise you will incinerate your fears—literally. It is helpful to complete this activity during one sitting, so prepare to have a fireplace, candle, or other burning facility available as well as paper and pen.

1. Consider the dreams, goals, and objectives you most want to accomplish. Write them down.

2. On a separate piece of paper, write down all the fears, hesitations, doubts, anxieties, and so on that cross your mind. Don't filter anything—just write.

3. If positive thoughts occur to you simultaneously, jot those down on a separate paper.

4. Keep writing until your mind is blank and you feel calm. You may even feel tired.

5. Look over your page of fears and doubts. Give them a label, such as "mind terrors," "brain bandits," or "energy divers."

6. If you can easily think of a positive response to these "brain bandits," write that on the page with your positive messages. If no responses come easily to mind, think of one positive thought, quote, or motto that can motivate you at this time. For example, "Knowing is not enough, we must apply; willing is not enough, we must do."[3]

---

3 Bruce Lee

7. With your positive thought firmly in mind, burn your page of negativity.

THE PROFUSION OF POTENTIAL

A subtle fear that can undermine your confidence is the sense that there isn't *enough* of something or there isn't enough for you. For the purposes of our work in this book, I want you to accept the concept that *you are enough*. You have the ability to do what you need to do, when you need to do it. If you are honest with yourself, you will find this to be true. You can count on yourself to do what you need to do. This is one way you can begin to fully trust yourself on this journey.

When you embrace this idea that you are enough, you realize you have the opportunity to fully appreciate and be grateful for all that exists. You find that everything you need truly does exist for you, without taking away from anyone else. You can accept life, enjoying the times when everything is in harmony and also release anxiety when everything seems in conflict, knowing you are still able to control some aspects of it. Keep these ideas in mind as you complete the following exercise.

EXERCISE THREE
HAVING IT ALL: THE LAW OF ABUNDANCE

1. Make a list of all the ways you are satisfied with yourself and your life in which you had some element of participation or control. Examples include the love of family or friends, the joy of dancing, the calm feeling you get every time you garden, and the total peace you feel

before falling asleep. Focus on how joyful and aligned you feel at the times you listed.

2. Next, make a list of all the things in your life that you are grateful for, whether you had anything to do with them or not. Examples could include the clean air you breathe, the dark green of fir trees, and your favorite restaurant's menu.

By focusing on how you *feel* when successful, you set yourself up for a positive outcome. The more frequently you encourage yourself and retrain your thoughts to focus on the feeling of obtaining success, the more adept you will be at overcoming doubts that arise. Keeping in mind all the things you are grateful for reminds your body of that positive response and trains it to expect that same response from experiences in life. True transformation, which is by definition *lasting* change, comes via incremental modifications that allow the brain to assimilate its capacity for new knowledge and adapt through neuroplasticity.[4]

DO THE STEPS—TAKE ACTION!

St. Francis of Assisi once said, "Start by doing what's necessary, then do what's possible; and suddenly you are doing the impossible." These words simplify and clarify life for me, and I hope you will find them inspirational.

You can analyze your feelings and think about what is happening, but until you put action behind your desires, you

---

4 Neuroplasticity refers to physical adaptations made in the brain to incorporate new pathways of behavior, thought, emotions, and formation of fresh neural patterns.

won't accomplish your dreams. There are many ways to set and achieve goals. All of them work—the trick is to *do* them and *follow through*. Some methods will feel more comfortable to each of us depending on our personal style. The Resources section has a variety of sources if you want to explore further options in goal setting. You can begin here.

EXERCISE FOUR
MAKE IT HAPPEN

1. Before capturing your dreams, goals, and objectives, reflect on why you want to reach that dream. Why is the goal important to you? What does it provide you when you achieve it? How will your life be different? Exactly what will your life feel like once your dream is real?

2. After you have integrated what this change will feel like, write down what you want to accomplish that is unique to you. See if any of the suggestions in the following list appeals to you or prompts your own ideas for writing down your goals.

   - If you're a list maker, make a list.

   - Prominently post photos representing your goals on a wall you see daily.

   - Use a whiteboard and dry erase markers for frequently updated dreams.

   - Make a sticker chart complete with benchmarks and rewards.

3. Break down the dreams into manageable chunks, small enough to be easily accomplished.

4. Utilize the SMART method. Design your goals using the following formula. Make them:

> **S** pecific
>
> **M** easurable
>
> **A** ctionable
>
> **R** elevant
>
> **T** ime-bound

5. Build in celebrations and rewards. Not only does this reinforce progress toward your goals, it also fortifies the concept of joy as a core principle in life, which we discuss later in this chapter.

6. Anticipate the journey, and thwart obstacles. Experience the journey through visualization—see and feel it step by step. When you encounter an obstacle, make note of it. If it has a possibility of happening, consider whether there is any action you can take now to prevent it from thwarting your progress.

7. Create an environment for success. Whatever will ensure a smoother path to your dreams, make that happen. Perhaps it's surrounding yourself with a support team or sending reinforcement messages via daily digital quotes or music. Maybe it's graphing out your journey visually.

Often we can be very adept at setting goals and organizing them, while simultaneously lacking the ability to connect our goals to their objective. Connor is a perfect example. He was a married, physically fit, accomplished young professional with two children under the age of five when he hired me to help him uncover his purpose, examine how it would unfold in his life, and develop tools to achieve it. Very organized and accountable, he already had goal systems in place and had read most of the latest inspirational and business titles. Looking at him, he appeared to already have his life and all components in order.

He told me he wanted to work on his goals, but couldn't say what his passions in life were. There was no connection between his goals and his inner pilot light. Our work began with rediscovery of his passions in life. We used those as a guiding light to drive and test his other ideas. When we focused on his values, Connor discovered he was driven by creativity, the need to leave a legacy, and the desire for open communication. Each fit into his current activities and shed light on why he felt so compelled to take action in his life.

A SOURCE OF DAILY DELIGHT

When we connect with joy, we are able to release fear. The two emotions cannot coexist. If you live life with joy as a base principle, you will systematically eliminate self-doubt and foster self-confidence, thereby automatically helping you reach your objectives.

Living life with joy as a core resilience, it is easy to understand and have the conviction that despite all else, life *is* good. You cannot control what happens to you, but you *can* control how you respond and choose to open your heart against all odds. By combining joy with the concept of abundance, you open up to the endless possibilities of what life has to offer your full potential and purpose. When your heart is open, joy can flood in. When your heart is closed, you are susceptible to fear and insecurity.

Governments, churches, and other organizations organize manifestos and creeds, stating the principles the organization lives by. That is also an excellent way to clarify what is critical to you in your life. You state your creed—your nonnegotiable criteria for the kind of life you will have—which helps you realign your physical criteria when they go off center.

You are already acting from your beliefs. As we discussed above, beliefs shape behaviors as our opinions and ideas guide our actions. Take control of which beliefs have the most power to support you in moving forward. Use the following exercise to solidify your strong foundation of beliefs now.

EXERCISE FIVE
YOUR PERSONAL CREED

Gather any materials you might want—art supplies, journal, and so on. Use your creativity as you construct your creed.

Give it a name that has power for you. Maybe it is "My Manifesto," "My Creed," "My Rules to Live By," or "My Nonnegotiables." Choose how you want to record it, but be sure it is in some form of a written list that can be easily referred to. You could include images plus text or just text. Take all the time you need and write down the principles of life that are the most important to you and that you will include from this day on. Be sure to include joy. If you need help getting started, here are some examples:

- I will incorporate creativity in my daily life.

- Physical health and wellness is a priority in my day.

- I will always make my best effort when I commit to something, even if I know the result will not meet my expectation. I will take satisfaction in doing my best.

- Laughter and joy will be part of my day, every day.

- Meditation and contemplation are a priority for me.

- I will spend time every day outside.

- My family and friends are more important than my possessions.

- Travel is imperative for broadening my perspective.

- I choose to let go of anxiety and self-doubt.

Examples of creeds include Lululemon's corporate manifesto,[5] Brené Brown's "10 Guideposts for Wholehearted Living,"[6] and the Seven Factors of Enlightenment in Buddhism.[7]

---

5 "The Lululemon Manifesto," http://www.lululemon.com/about/manifesto

6 Brené Brown, *Daring Greatly: How the Courage to Be Vulnerable Transforms the Way We Live, Love, Parent and Lead* (New York: Penguin, 2012) p. 9.

7 Geri Larkin, *Close to the Ground: Reflections on the Seven Factors of Enlightenment* (Berkeley: Rodmell Press, 2013).

Trust forward to live your purpose! We are forming an alignment between body, mind, and spirit—a cohesion between values and behavior and an alignment of intention and purpose with action. Be accountable for owning your life's direction, and gain control by prevailing over fear.

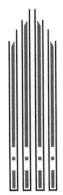

chapter two

Define Your Values: What Do You Stand For?

Love is the affinity which links and draws together the elements of the world...Love, in fact, is the agent of universal synthesis...[It] is a sacred reserve of energy; it is like the blood of spiritual evolution.

—TEILHARD DE CHARDIN

Our core values are those principles we hold most dear—the beliefs that govern our behavior and rule our lives. They are the fundamentals over which wars are fought, lives are lost, and love is won. We know what our values are, but it is crucial that we are able to clearly articulate them in order to use them as a foundation for our life work. In this chapter, we work on identifying our values; in the next chapter, we work on defining our life purpose. These two elements together—values and life purpose—are the foundation of our alignment.

From our values we can establish a code of personal ethics that transcends all situations and circumstances and applies universally and impartially in all conditions. We use our personal convictions to apply our own moral code and create a reality that is both meaningful and practical. Because values connect with our personal identity, they are the glue of the alignment to our authentic self. They become our litmus test for what we truly believe and what beliefs we are willing to put into action. They define who we are and what we stand for. They are our internal guidance system that helps us make better decisions.

We instinctively understand this, but articulating it is more challenging. Terminology of strengths and values are often erroneously interchanged. Strengths and values differ in a significant way: we *choose* our values, whereas our strengths are inherent traits that cause us to excel in a particular fashion. After we've defined what our key principles in life are, we can then clearly express them; it becomes effortless to stand by them and to stay in moral alignment. One way to define our values is by tuning into our heart's intelligence.

Our heart is reputed as an independent source of intelligence by an increasing number of scientists. Researchers at the nonprofit Institute of HeartMath studied the science of the heart and found that measurable cardio-electromagnetic fields can be detected between human bodies, showing that intelligence is not restricted to the brain but is much more widely distributed in our bodies. Three main locations of intelligence are the brain, the heart, and the stomach, each with its own specific characteristics.[8]

The heart's intelligence differs from the intelligence we gain from the brain or stomach. The heart directs us to what we truly need to know for our happiness in life, our soul's purpose, and our larger goals. Intuitively, this is something we already know and may be tapping into. Expressions such as "what does your heart tell you?" and "change of heart" are indications that we are well aware the heart has wisdom to share. It is our heart that helps us examine our values.

---

8 HeartMath Institute, www.heartmath.org

The heart responds to intuition and reflection. In order to tap into this reserve and understand what values and themes are important in your life, the exercise below will help you focus on what matters most to you.

EXERCISE ONE
YOUR CORE VALUES

1. Reflect on "What's important to me?" What, above all else, do you care about? Put routine thoughts of career, family, home, and responsibilities to the side and just consider what remains critical to you in your life.

2. Look at the following list, and mark the 20 values that hold the most significance to you. If you think of a word that better expresses how you feel, write it in.

3. From those 20, identify whether there are any themes among them. For example, do you have communication, service, and coaching/mentoring? Those could be grouped into a theme of coaching/mentoring.

4. After identifying any themes, reduce the list to ten items.

5. From the list of ten, choose your top three core values.

6. Reflect on whether the values you chose show up in your life through your actions.

CORE VALUES					
account-ability	compassion	entrepre-neurial	generosity	openness	self-disci-pline
achieve-ment	competence	environ-mental	health	patience	teamwork

CORE VALUES					
adaptability	conflict resolution	awareness	humility	persever-ance	trust
ambition	continuous learning	ethics	humor/fun	personal fulfillment	vision
balance (home/ work)	courage	excellence	indepen-dence	personal growth	wealth
being the best	creativity	fairness	initiative	profes-sional growth	well-being (physical, emotional, mental, spiritual)
caring	dialogue (or communi-cation)	family	integrity	recognition	wisdom
clarity	ease with uncertainty	financial stability	job security	reliability	loyalty
coaching/ mentoring	efficiency	forgiveness	leadership	respect	prestige
commit-ment	enthu-siasm/ positive attitude	friendship	listening	risk-taking	power
community involvement	future gen-erations/ legacy	making a difference	safety/ security	interdepen-dence	innovation

EXERCISE TWO
PERSONAL VALUES ASSESSMENT

Go to www.valuescentre.com for a free, web-based Personal Values Assessment.

As you do the exercise, don't confuse your core values with what gives you a sense of self-worth. Sometimes we set goals to provide a sense of self-worth, and if we don't reach our objective, we interpret the nonarrival as failure rather than a technical difficulty, a misaligned route, or a setback. Failure is giving up. In contrast, a mistake or setback is far from a failure. It is just information gained from which to move forward. If you choose to give up entirely, you've surrendered the opportunity to learn. Setbacks are reminders to pay attention to what is and isn't working and to readjust for the optimal outcome.

To distinguish between your core values and your sense of value, tune into your heart once again to decide what the motivating element is that drives you forward in life. Those motivating elements are the core values.

Whether we are conscious of it or not, all of our decisions on how we spend our time come from our values. By living a values-driven life, we consciously create our reality rather than allowing circumstances to direct us. There is a subtle difference between living our life intentionally and allowing circumstances to drive us when the activities may be the same.

Dan illustrates someone who intentionally changed his approach with satisfying results. Dan had accomplished great things in life: building a community center, placing in his age category in local 10k races, coaching a boy's soccer team to state finals, rising to the rank of executive in his profession, and being acknowledged by his friends as a gourmet cook. Yet Dan consistently felt unfulfilled and aimless despite all his time spent on what would be considered meaningful activities.

After consulting with him, it was clear he wasn't aware of his own achievements and talents in any significant way. He moved from one activity to the next depending on who asked him to do what he felt he was able to do.

Dan and I worked together clarifying and articulating his core values, delineating what his core values were, and separating them from what gave him a reinforcing sense of value. Once he could focus on reinforcing his core values and intrinsically building his sense of self-satisfaction, he was able to determine more clearly which activities would be the most rewarding for him.

Once he saw the reinforcement of his decisions, he began to get enthusiastic about them again. Connection with others was critical for him to feel fulfilled. He developed deeper and more extensive communication skills, which allowed him to overcome his hesitation in sharing his goals and dreams. This then led to even deeper connections with others.

In the end, Dan's activities didn't change and neither did his values. What changed was his awareness of his driving principles in life and his dedication to set his life in accordance with them. The deep feeling of self-worth that grew as a result of that was permanent because he was living in alignment with who he was.

Understanding the importance of honoring who we are and what we stand for is one way of taking control of our world. We build a feeling of self-worth by keeping agreements we make to ourselves. Consciously choosing to see significance in our personal achievements, having friends who make us better people, and choosing how we are going to present ourselves each day help align us with our values and reinforce our core identity.

The things we own, the places we live, and the people we associate with all represent key elements of ourselves and our iden-tities because they enrich our lives by varying degrees. The closer each one aligns with our core values determines their specific significance to us.

Similarly, your day, the time you spend, and the places in which you operate should all reflect what is important to you. Your values are the driving principles of your life, reflected in your activities. Make sure you are filling your day with people, places, and things that really matter to you. The exercise below will help you clarify where to spend the majority of your time.

EXERCISE THREE
MATCH YOUR DAY TO YOUR VALUES

1. Write out a sample day's routine, including typical clothing worn, dietary regime, routines, people seen, and so on.

2. Reflect on your behaviors and activities during that typical day.

3. Look back over your list of core values and determine whether your routines are reinforcing your values.

4. Among your behaviors on this day, decide where you can give up time, activities, and so on.

5. Focus on the areas that highlight your values and match your behaviors to them, allocating the majority of your time there.

Once we understand what our values are, we can more easily put the pieces of our lives in place by evaluating every object, thought, word, and action and asking ourselves how closely it aligns with us. During the course of a day, we can take a moment to consider whether something we are doing or someone we are spending time with helps us be a better version of ourselves or not. If we are living with our values, there's a sense of all being right with the world.

When we let ourselves down by not meeting our agreements or living up to our standards, we can feel it in the pit of our stomach. Our stomach intelligence houses over 100 million neurons that signal emotional responses giving us clues when something is wrong or right.[9]

Staying in alignment with our values can become an easy, calming, and automatic process. We have an internal resource to tap into as a guidepost. We can check into our heart, stomach, and head instantaneously to keep us in check and in alignment.

Audrey is a great example of this. She had experienced major life transitions when she began working with me. A corporate auditor, she was going through the brave actions of recreating life after the death of a young son but lacked any reassurance that she was doing the right things.

After clarifying what her core values were, we worked together to chart Audrey's year ahead, combining milestones, goals, and dreams on one plan. Using her well-developed analytical skills, Audrey then separated her year into months and considered each block of time. This is where she froze.

Her breathing became noticeably shallow. Later she confided that all the entries on paper just looked like scribbles of ink. I asked if for the purpose of the exercise we could think of it as just

---

9 Adam Hadhazy, "Think Twice: How the Gut's 'Second Brain' Influences Mood and Well-Being," February 12, 2010, http://www.scientificamerican.com/article/gut-second-brain/.

another work project instead of as her life. Audrey was then able to break each month into weeks and then into tasks, and we built a comprehensive road map using Audrey's intellectual skills.

That looked great on paper, but it wasn't going to get Audrey any further in her life. The next step we took was to do an exercise where we checked in with Audrey's heart and stomach on each item. Now we started to make progress. As she got more information, she felt more comfortable and was able to make adjustments to her plan.

From that point on, she was able to use a quick version of the exercise to check in with herself and stay in alignment. It's been nine years since the death of her son, and Audrey felt so comfortable with the process that she has gone on to create her second road map using the same process.

The following exercise, adapted from *Create a World That Works: Tools for Personal and Global Transformation* by Alan Seale, is useful for identifying and checking in with the three intelligences.

EXERCISE FOUR
THREE INTELLIGENCES

Sit where you will be comfortable and undisturbed. Take in several deep, calming breaths to clear your mind of any thoughts you might have of the day. As you begin to relax, bring to mind the topic or situation you'd like to have considered by your three intelligences.

1. Starting with your heart, breathe, relax, and wait. What does your heart have to tell you?

2. Moving to your stomach, breathe, relax, and wait. What does your gut have to tell you?

3. Shifting to your head, breathe, relax, and wait. What does your head say?

Do any of the three intelligences want to say something to another? Keep listening until you feel completely calm.

When you have gotten some helpful insights, breathe, slowly open your eyes, and write down anything you want to remember later.

The exercise gets easier the more you practice it and is immensely helpful to use going forward with all your projects and goals. It is a quick yet profound way to stay aligned with what is most meaningful to you and to move forward for full-spectrum living. It has the additional benefits of building your self-confidence as you build credence in your thoughts and actions, while simultaneously being relaxing and motivating for you.

The expression of our values takes on various forms, particularly as our values shift and deepen through life. But if we continue to steer from our internal key values, any external reactions won't impact us. We may still feel disappointed when others don't share our excitement, but it doesn't result in questioning our self-worth, because we already hold our principles in high regard and protect them. We can't be deterred from moving forward in life. Our actions are driven from integrity. We are living consistently within our particular alignment of thoughts, words, and behaviors, all propelled from a much deeper source.

Conversely, if we watch for others to respond to our actions and look for approval, we are subject to *their* moods and morals rather than holding our own foremost. This is how we can distinguish between being motivated to act from our *core values* as opposed to looking for a *sense of value*. When we align our world with our values, everything, everyone, and every action is in accord with what is most significant to us.

When we intentionally fill our life with choices that inspire us to be the best version of ourselves, we are accepting our role to live our purpose in life. We become receptive to a much larger process of life. Values remain our constant litmus test of integrity. In the same way that they reinforce our own internal feeling of authenticity, values make it clear to others who we are and what we stand for.

Combine your life purpose with your values and well, that's an unstoppable combination. Let's take a look at how that can happen.

chapter three

Find Your Purpose: Allow Yourself to Be Seen

That luminous part of you that exists beyond personality—
your soul, if you will—is as bright and shining as any that
has ever been...Clear away everything that keeps you separate
from this secret luminous peace...share its fruits tirelessly.

—GEORGE SAUNDERS

Just as values are our internal driving system compelling us to act, our life **purpose** propels us to *want* to act. It gives us the *why* behind getting up every morning and provides the enthusiastic answer to "*What difference does it make?*" Getting up makes a difference because we all have a purpose in life to live; *we* make a difference and until we are fulfilling our unique purpose, we aren't taking advantage of the greatest happiness available to us. Our purpose is our raison d'être—our reason for being. Why wouldn't we go to the effort to figure this out when aligning our values and purpose leads to enduring peace of mind?

Our life **mission** is the actual work that we do to fulfill our purpose. To accept ourselves as individuals with a unique purpose, combined with all our gifts and imperfections, is our ultimate objective. Once we begin to value the mission that we have and the work we do and see these things as larger than ourselves, we can then begin to accept that our love and appreciation for ourselves stems from a deeper universal love for all mankind. Our life vision is this wide worldview: the concept of life is so much larger than ourselves.

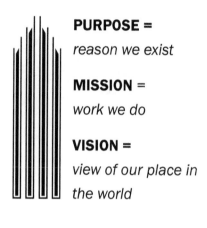

PURPOSE =

reason we exist

MISSION =

work we do

VISION =

view of our place in the world

When we have concurrence between these three components—our life purpose, life mission, and life vision—our days are full of new energy even though we may be doing the same routines we've always done. And if you don't yet know your life purpose, figuring it out will give all the peace of mind, enthusiasm, and energy you were searching for. With all that available to you, why wouldn't you do it?

Start by letting go of all disappointments from past efforts. Letting go of judgment is the first step to total acceptance of our humanity. It sets the stage to allow us to see our full potential and have a lot of fun in the process. Decisions come later. For now, just open up and allow some possibilities. At this stage, there is no room for feeling guilt, shame, or self-blame over the past.

To completely let go of any past regrets that prevent us from moving forward, we have to first learn to understand how to forgive ourselves for anything we think isn't quite right. As we understand that, we begin to feel the compassion that comes from knowing the pain of feeling separate and divided is a choice. And because it is a choice, it is within our power to change it!

When we begin to accept that, we begin to reclaim our power and start to feel our energy return. We start by accepting that there is another way of thinking, then acting. Once we are encouraged by our results, enthusiasm builds, and it becomes easier to be compassionate, understanding that we are all united in our individual attempts of humanity. We each have our own way, and it is human to make choices we sometimes wish we hadn't.

Transformation and success happen through acknowledging without shame what truly exists, owning the reality of the situation, and handling whatever obstacles are in the way. When we live consciously, taking action will quickly improve the situation at hand. This allows even the harshest circumstances to become a crossroads for understanding, as we proactively create something out of them.

When life is in synch with who you are, you are able to meet all your responsibilities and commitments, excelling at them because of the enjoyment they provide, and still have time for the things, people, animals, activities, and places in life that are important to you. Finding your purpose is first knowing what those items of importance are.

How do we find our purpose? While our interests, goals, and passions can certainly be a part of finding our purpose, they are not in and of themselves our mission in life. Those items of importance are insightful clues, however. Remember, our mission is *how* we live our purpose. The following two exercises will help build toward the end exercise of writing your life purpose.

EXERCISE ONE
CALLING...ME

Write down adjectives describing:

1. Who I want to be

2. How I want to be known

3. How I would like others to describe me

Also, have someone else make a list of adjectives of you. (Choose who you ask carefully!)

You can jot down individual adjectives, full sentences, or phrases—whatever best expresses you. For example:

1. Who do I want to be? ...someone who is creative, patient, accepting of others, witty, quick thinking, etc.

2. How do I want to be known? ...as shocking, intelligent, funny, etc.

3. How would I like others to describe me? ...as complex, approachable, raising the standard, etc.

All the exercises in the book are intended to open your creative passageways, so write down the obvious thoughts and then keep going. Have fun, be daring, and don't hold back. You're not being graded on what you've written, so feel free to be uninhibited.

Take as much time as you need to fulfill this exercise—until you feel done. It can be extremely helpful to write everything down that you can possibly imagine and then let it sit. Go back to it as more thoughts percolate.

If you have trouble dreaming the big picture, see chapter 8, Visualizations and Meditations: Aid for Alignment, to open your intuition. Then revisit these exercises. You can also explore the Intuition Openers below. Once we loosen up the unconscious part of our brain, our creativity can freely circulate.

INTUITION OPENERS

Sometimes we have to calm down our conscious mind in order to open up the quieter, wiser subconscious mind and allow it to surface. Here are a few ways to open up the subconscious.[10]

- Take time to meditate or do some visualization exercises.

- Spend time outdoors in nature.

- Practice some silence every day.

- Do one activity, or more, just for the joy of it. Have ... pure ... fun! Take a break, and LAUGH!

- Write in a journal daily. For example, you might enter your thought or question, pause for an answer, and record what comes up.

- Make a note of your dreams.

- Exercise, preferably in the fresh air.

10 Adapted from http://www.yourtango.com/experts/jan-bowen/ 6-easy-ways-be-your-own-damn-therapist-with-confidenceyourtango articles, and syndicated in www.ThoughtCatalog.com (http://thoughtcatalog.com/jan-bowen/2015/05/6-simple-ways-to-sharpen-your-intuition-and-listen-to-what-that-inner-voice-is-telling-you/).

EXERCISE TWO
TRACKING...ME

Track your activities for a day/week/month.

- Note what is working well for you.

- Note what isn't working well.

- Note what changes you would like to make.

After conducting the above exercise, complete the Wheel of Life on page 53.

Just as you did in the first exercise, take your time writing, relaxing, having fun, and being creative. When you complete these exercises, you should feel that while they've taken some time, you have fresh insight and are really excited by some ideas, while also really surprised by some thoughts that have never occurred to you before. If you are lacking that level of enthusiasm, take a break, consider the Intuition Openers, and dream a bigger dream before continuing.

THE WHEEL OF LIFE

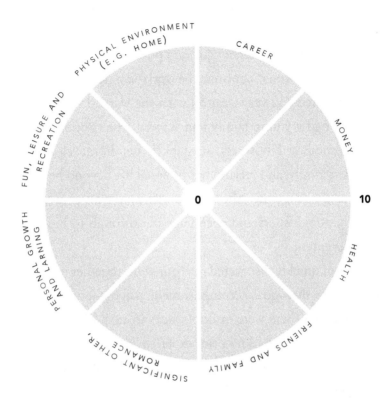

WHEEL OF LIFE INSTRUCTIONS

The 8 sections in the Wheel of Life represent balance.

- Please change, split or rename any category so that it's meaningful and represents a balanced life for you.

- Next, using the center of the wheel as 0 and the outer edge as 10, rank your level of satisfaction with each area out of 10 by drawing a straight or curved line to create a new outer edge (see example).

- The new perimeter of the circle represents your 'Wheel of Life'. Is it a bumpy ride?

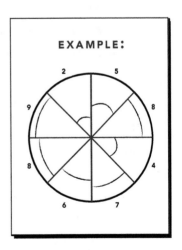

EXAMPLE:

When I speak with clients about their dreams and objectives, I often have them do exercises similar to the ones in this book. When one client, Carol, began working with me, she had already been to several life coaches with very positive results. Her expectation was that I would continue the work on a new set of goals. She was motivated and very clear on what she wanted to accomplish.

She had a young family and wanted to transition her career to a home-based business, reestablish her home closer to her extended family, and reclaim her personal life beyond being a new mom and young wife. She wanted someone who could help her with the tough spots and encourage her through to higher levels of achievement.

Carol quickly discovered that our work together was destined to be more than goal accomplishment when she undertook the first exercise. There were multiple steps in each of her objectives, most of which she had no prior experience with.

Enthusiastic and positive, when I gave her a reflective life questionnaire to ponder, she sent me an insightful email two days later. While she had been prepared to tackle her goals, she hadn't expected to encounter her deeper self, and that is what she found when she began her reflection and writing.

Over the course of two years, we *did* work on her goals, and she surpassed them all. But what she accomplished was far greater than that. She came to know her values and her life purpose. Her life purpose is to show young families that it is possible to live a good life. Her mission is to teach young inner-city families how to establish healthy eating habits despite any limitations they might have. While she is enjoying this stage of life, she is already anticipating that she will be enjoying the future ones as well.

The exercises you have done provide an insight on the external you that the world sees. Understanding your purpose entails paying attention to the input that surrounds you. Everyone in our lives serves as our teacher. They are mirrors of a sort, reflecting back our behaviors, providing lessons and opportunities from which we can benefit. If you don't like what you see, determine if it is because someone is acting in a way you would secretly like to or if someone is acting in the same manner you do and you don't like it!

The people in our life are clues for us, providing us with insight and a peek into alternative ways of being. These teachers are there whether we choose to see and accept their message or not. It's up to you whether you want to explore the meaning that your relationships have in your life. I encourage you to focus on at least your closest friends and family for invaluable insight on what makes you tick.

Because we are surrounded by stimuli constantly, our day-to-day experience can be overwhelming. All too often, it's tempting to deaden ourselves through drugs, food, or other means to shut down our brain and our emotions. But we aren't shutting the life lessons out. They don't go away—they just wind up tamped out momentarily.

Jake spent years shutting out input from everyone around him. He considered himself a happily married man, although his wife didn't share that impression. A successful business owner, Jake reveled in both his work and his hobbies. His family was a reflection of all his accomplishments, and his actions toward them were most often tied to other objectives. Family travel would be for a work conference; vacations were planned around his passion for race car driving. His home showcased his business achievements, complete with a professional kitchen for entertaining his clients and a home office that displayed his achievements and trophies.

All of these actions in themselves are fine. The fallout of Jake's intense focus was his family and social circle. Initially, just being together and sharing each other's company was enough. But Jake lacked consideration for those around him, and as the years went on, everyone developed individual interests and had their own achievements.

Jake's wife, Louise, an accomplished leader in her own right, would have been happy if she had been part of their life planning process or if her achievements within her field of education had been incorporated. She had a brilliant life purpose of her own and was successfully pursuing her life mission without his notice. Jake's sons became highly respected track and soccer stars.

Jake set up his life to be the central star in a cast of players rather than allowing each member to shine with their own talents. In the process, he risked losing everything as they gradually lost interest and patience in their supporting roles.

Louise and the boys were not silent through the years. They spoke up, but Jake didn't hear them. He continued to race cars, build his business, and look to the external signs of accomplishment as reassurance that he had everything he wanted. He was numbing himself to what was continually being presented to him.

Jake's wake-up call came when Louise had an opportunity to be president of a small college across the country. She was willing to negotiate and accommodate many details of the arrangement to make it work for the entire family, without anyone having to give up what was important to them. But Jake couldn't see that. He set an ultimatum that Louise could choose the job or him. She chose the job.

Jake didn't see that possibility coming, and he was shaken to the core when it happened. For the first time, he saw his family for who they were. It took almost a year, and many heart-wrenching hours, for Jake to accept himself and his family as they were and then to make changes in how he approached life. It wasn't easy for him, but it was beneficial and gratifying.

He now knows that he has always had everything he wanted but needed to open his eyes to how he approached his life. In the process, he saw that his life purpose was to lead his life with integrity, using his resources to make a positive difference in the lives of others and offering support to others whenever possible.

The path he had been on was designed to show him that a redirection was needed. When he looked back, however, he could see that throughout his life, sharing his resources and knowledge was the common denominator that gave him joy and purpose while enriching others.

We hear and see when we are ready, and we do so in the way that makes sense to us. Every person's individual skill and ability set is not immediately available to all—whoever we truly are in our nature is intended to be shared.

To live each day fully means allowing ourselves to be seen when we succeed *and* when we fall short. When we decide to readily give the talents we have, the enjoyment in participating with others and in knowing we are fulfilling our life purpose is far greater than expected.

The irony of our unique traits is that our own skills are so crystal clear and natural precisely because they are ours. They are in fact our second nature. They are so obvious to us that we tend to overlook them. Yet others benefit from us using them and are drawn to us specifically in order for us to use these skills. That is one way in which we can understand what our unique characteristics are and is often an excellent indication of our life purpose. The next exercise illustrates this by revealing the intersection between what your desires are and how others see you.

EXERCISE THREE
THE SWEET SPOT

1. Draw three intersecting circles, as illustrated below. Each circle represents one of the following:

   - Circle (a) what you're good at

   - Circle (b) what you love doing

   - Circle (c) what others ask of you or your thoughts of what the world needs.

2. For the topic of each circle, list all the things that come to mind for each category. Have fun, and be CREATIVE with this! Write fast, and write often. Make a list and put it down, and then pick it up later when more ideas come to you. Write in the morning or late at night, or record ideas into your phone. Don't hold back! This is where your intuitive mind will give you information to build from.

3. Once you've spent some time on all three circles, consider asking others their thoughts. Ask a friend or coworker what they think your greatest strength is, and the answer just might surprise you. Rather than hearing

"determination," you might hear "sense of humor." Record it all, and judge nothing. If I haven't said it before, HAVE FUN with this!

The intersection of the circles is known as the "sweet spot." Consider whether what shows up there sounds like your life purpose.

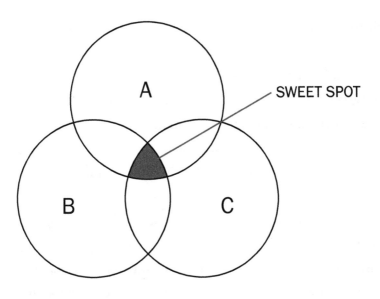

Not showing yourself as you fully are with your thoughts, beliefs, and preferences robs you and drains you. Your essence consists of your gifts and your reason for being on this earth—it is your unique reason for being here that you alone can do. We are each composed of a unique equation. It is up to us to revel in that equation and to share it in the world. Before we can do that comfortably, we need to feel safe.

We choose the people we associate with for a variety of reasons, among them being a sense of safety and comfort in their company. Beyond the emotional comfort we gain with our friends, brain research shows we are registering a matching neural action, which creates empathy. "[Mirror neurons]...are triggered both when performing an action and when observing another individual performing the same action...[They] therefore allow us to realize what others are doing and understand their intentions, for the very reason that they allow us to experience what we are observing firsthand, as if we were performing that action ourself."[11] This is one more reason our relationships have so much to teach us.

But it is up to us ultimately to create the feeling of safety for ourselves. Do this by observing those around you, reflecting on your observations, noticing any modifications you might want to make, and then taking positive steps toward your own purpose. The example of how Jake modified his life is an illustration of how to do this.

It helps if you understand yourself well, so taking time to do the things that bring you joy only furthers your purpose. Enjoyment is never a waste of time. If you ever needed a reason to make leisure or vacation time a priority, consider it a tool to fully understand your life purpose.

Infuse everything you do with your own brand of brilliance. If you have a sparkling sense of humor, make your work funny. If aesthetics matter to you, make everything you touch beautiful in its own way. If you value family above all else, make sure you have

---

11 Matteo Rizzato, "Mirror Neurons and Empathy: Experiencing Another's Inner World with Clarity Instead of Fear," *Elephant*, December 2, 2014, http://www.elephantjournal.com/2014/12/mirror-neurons-empathy-experiencing-anothers-inner-world-with-clarity-instead-of-fear/.

your family represented in all aspects of your life. If you don't have a family, create one!

EXERCISE FOUR
UNVEIL YOURSELF!

Look for clues that already exist. If you like games, you'll like the exploration in this exercise. Investigate as many of the following suggestions that sound intriguing to you.

The crucial component in this exercise is to pay attention to when you are intrigued by the response you receive. The power lies in how you hear the message. When that happens, write it down or record it! Preserve it in some way because it's important!

- What is the ancient meaning of your name? How does that relate to how you are now known?

- What is the specific astrological chart you came to this earth with? What tools were you given by the stars to accomplish your work? Reflect on how this has shown up throughout your life. If this intrigues you, have a reading by a professional astrologer.

- What does the numerology of your life reveal? How has this been true in various chapters of your life?

- Get a professional tarot, intuitive, or palm reading. Listen to the information given, and pay attention to what might grab your attention in a powerful way. Reflect on how that might have meaning and application in your life.

Remember your power and potential. Where you are now is not where you will always be if you don't intend it to be so. Everything we do *is* a reflection of our values and originality. So allow change, and value your significance.

Pay attention to those clear thoughts that repeat and fill you with conviction and energy. Write them down. Those are your guiding clues to what is important. They won't quiet or go away until they are paid attention to. We never have to surrender what makes us truly happy as we fulfill our life purpose.

Your purpose doesn't change throughout your life, but it does evolve, and the mechanics of *how* you fulfill your mission at times will vary. How your purpose is expressed when you are young may differ from what you do as an adult. Some of the changes along the way are building blocks to how we ultimately express our life purpose. These building blocks all connect and lead us to deeper expressions of our purpose, as they did for another client of mine that we'll call Elaine.

Elaine's life purpose has always been to teach others, and although she sometimes struggled with this, she always incorporated some aspect of teaching into her life. During her corporate career, although her position didn't require it, Elaine integrated various training programs for internal and external clients. Now in her late 60s, she has redirected her path a little; she works as a consultant to foreign governments, advising them in their negotiations with corporate entities. It sounds like a big shift, but she is essentially teaching them how to communicate across all lines of functionality and nationality—something at which she is innately skilled.

Our purpose is never to be less than we are but instead to come to full fruition of our own power with the deepest understanding of how to interact with another's path. Living life in a smaller role than who you are serves no benefit other than to make yourself and those around you uncomfortable.

First, you create your world where you can be content. Then you can invite others in and allow them to have the world they have created. When two worlds combine with self-actualized individuals, you're experiencing the sweet spot where you are serving a greater good by fully being yourself. Once we allow ourselves to be seen and are comfortable with it, we can welcome it.

Human beings are constructed brilliantly of Body, Mind, and Spirit, all working in concert. Remember the Three Intelligences exercise from the previous chapter? All these components of ourselves work together to help us not only live our life purpose but to figure it out in the first place.

The ego, though often maligned, is a brilliant tool in accomplishing our purpose. It is our arms and legs in accomplishing the work, but it cannot be relegated as just the mechanical means to an end or we risk imploding before we reach full expression of self. If we allow our soul to direct our actions and the ego to be the proverbial muscle, working in tangent while accepting all they discover along the way, we have the equation of wholeness. The soul allows the ego to bring lessons and opportunities to it, illuminating potential self-limiting behavior and offering circumstances for even deeper insight.

We balance the unique gifts and talents we are given with the powerful abilities the ego provides us, mix them with truth, and allow that alchemy to form an outward presence for the world to appreciate. This is our goal—to allow our unique light to shine brightly outward, illuminating all we do and radiating on everyone who is around us. We each live our purpose while appreciating each other's contributions. The collective effort toward whole-hearted full-spectrum living is what moves us as a society forward.

EXERCISE FIVE
DEFINE YOUR LIFE PURPOSE

Write your Life Mission. Include your Life Vision.

You've gathered all the data you need and hopefully spent the time necessary reflecting on the input to be able to capture your life purpose.

Now, record your answers to the following questions. They will lead to and build upon each other.

- Why do you get up in the morning? What is your **core motivation**? (Refer to your core values if you need help answering this.)

- What do you see as your **internal** motivation for your **purpose**? Why?

- What do you see as your **internal** motivation for your **life vision**? Why?

- What do you see as your **external** motivation for your **life vision**? Why?

- What do you see as your **external** motivation for your **purpose**? Why?

Reflect on your answers. In no more than five sentences, write your life vision to clarify your perspective of your life's role. If it is helpful, use any of the phrases below to craft your mission statement, declaring how you intend to act on your life purpose. Edit it until the statements completely represent you.

- To [verb/what you want to be] so that [your life accomplishment]...

- To develop [qualities] so that [purpose]...

- To live each day with [driving passion] so that [purposeful conclusion]...

Some examples:

- To teach my knowledge so that others can fully realize their potential.

- To live my life dedicated to stomping out guilt and pain over grief and serve as an advocate for survivors' rights so that survivors can go on to a brighter future.

- To make a difference showing patients they can be beautiful through life-threatening illnesses so that they can feel some peace and hope on a daily basis.

- To serve as a mentor to younger individuals, helping them fully develop into their full potential in life.

Success, when propelled from our values, feels differently from being successful from an ego standpoint. When driven from our purpose, success is no longer solely results driven. Therefore, the outcome of our effort doesn't have a win/lose monitor but becomes an evaluation tool for us to determine if we were on point with our intention.

Our emotions, heart-fueled, are our guideposts. They show us where our passion in life can be found and where we can refuel. They show up in our daily life through our relationships, in our dreams, in the themes of the books we read, in the music we listen to, and even in the places of tension in our body. See Emotional Centers of Body chart on the following page. The ability to identify, translate, and then manage and integrate emotions in a proactive manner is emotional intelligence. Emotional intelligence entails distinguishing between one's own emotions and another's and identifying and setting boundaries appropriately, all with the purpose of living a fully integrated, aligned, purposeful, conscious life.

Our feelings are a decisive monitor, indicating when we are within alignment and when we need to examine and adjust. As humans we like to exist within a comfort zone. Our feelings subtly guide and teach us the distinction between healthy comfort and comfort that reinforces avoidance. Successful alignment is a balance with our life purpose that incorporates our values, is driven by the ego, and is reinforced through our emotions.

EMOTIONAL ENERGY CENTERS OF THE BODY

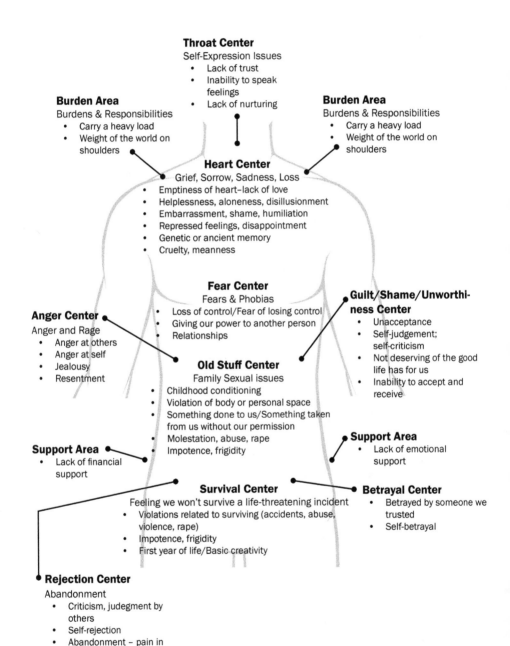

Throat Center
Self-Expression Issues
- Lack of trust
- Inability to speak feelings
- Lack of nurturing

Burden Area
Burdens & Responsibilities
- Carry a heavy load
- Weight of the world on shoulders

Burden Area
Burdens & Responsibilities
- Carry a heavy load
- Weight of the world on shoulders

Heart Center
Grief, Sorrow, Sadness, Loss
- Emptiness of heart–lack of love
- Helplessness, aloneness, disillusionment
- Embarrassment, shame, humiliation
- Repressed feelings, disappointment
- Genetic or ancient memory
- Cruelty, meanness

Fear Center
Fears & Phobias
- Loss of control/Fear of losing control
- Giving our power to another person
- Relationships

Guilt/Shame/Unworthiness Center
- Unacceptance
- Self-judgement; self-criticism
- Not deserving of the good life has for us
- Inability to accept and receive

Anger Center
Anger and Rage
- Anger at others
- Anger at self
- Jealousy
- Resentment

Old Stuff Center
Family Sexual issues
- Childhood conditioning
- Violation of body or personal space
- Something done to us/Something taken from us without our permission
- Molestation, abuse, rape
- Impotence, frigidity

Support Area
- Lack of financial support

Support Area
- Lack of emotional support

Survival Center
Feeling we won't survive a life-threatening incident
- Violations related to surviving (accidents, abuse, violence, rape)
- Impotence, frigidity
- First year of life/Basic creativity

Betrayal Center
- Betrayed by someone we trusted
- Self-betrayal

Rejection Center
Abandonment
- Criticism, judgment by others
- Self-rejection
- Abandonment – pain in the heart

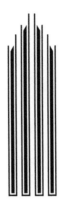

part two

THE TEMPLATE

Establishing Your Personal Template

A musician must make music, an artist must paint, a poet
must write, if he is to be ultimately at peace with himself... We
fear to know the fearsome and unsavory aspects of ourselves,
but we fear even more to know the godlike in ourselves.

—ABRAHAM MASLOW

Your Personal Template is a comprehensive supply of resources, a compendium compiled specifically for your individual needs that you use to stay aligned to function at your optimum effectiveness. It is a well of personal ingenuity, inventiveness, and creativity to inspire, refresh, and motivate you.

Its main purpose is to give you a set of options to help you establish and maintain alignment of your total self—body, mind, and spirit. So often, it is easy to become focused on just one aspect of life and get out of balance. When that happens, we are like a wobbly wheel, no longer able to sustain smooth momentum to confidently live our purpose with integrity or even just to enjoy our life.

Your tools of alignment are composed of your Daily Practice, your Structure of Tactics, and a Bundle of Exceptional Resources. The next three chapters will discuss each in detail and help you incorporate them into your life.

To realign, different elements of our Template are used at various times, just as various strategies are used comprehensively to align and accomplish objectives. And consistent with any strategic plan, your activities and processes will vary. If you find yourself changing through the years, your strategies will also change. Our Template, though, becomes part of us as we move forward through all parts of life. Two primary pieces—the Daily Practice and our Structure of Tactics—are daily efforts. We use the Bundle of Exceptional Resources as needed.

The critical element that makes our Template work is that we choose our individual game plan, and it is uniquely ours. There is no universal answer or one size fits all. Just as an artisan or apprentice takes satisfaction in learning their art, so should you. Many resource options are listed in the following exercises, and they are a small sampling of what's available. Take the time to choose the precise ones that function best for you.

Your Template will evolve through the years, but it needs to be grounded in the three cornerstones of Body, Mind, and Spirit. Therefore, how you compose these modules is crucial. By constructing them to match your particular needs and adjusting them as necessary, you will ensure you have the right tools.

If you would prefer to download the entire Template
ToolKit, I've made the resources available to you at
www.ItsNotThatComplicatedToolKit.com.

Create a Daily Practice

But little by little, as you left their voices behind, the stars
began to burn through the sheets of clouds, and there was a
new voice, which you slowly recognized as your own...

—MARY OLIVER, *THE JOURNEY*

A Daily Practice is a routine we establish for ourselves that brings all the parts of our life into alignment to support us as we live our purpose and values. It is a discipline we do each and every day. By committing to taking routine action daily, we set a clear statement that our life is important and that *we* are important. Moreover, a Daily Practice enables you to accumulate simple, positive habits that result in powerful results. This pattern leads to successful alignment.

Although some people may shy away from the term "soul," our Daily Practice is housekeeping for our soul. Remember that our life purpose entails pursuing things greater than ourselves. Tending to that greater part of us through our Daily Practice is what keeps us clear enough to keep living with integrity.

To live a full-spectrum life with integrity, we need a Daily Practice to keep us clear on our values and priorities and to remind us of them repeatedly. Without this daily routine, the alignment of our life gets quite precarious at times. With it, life seems very manageable, and days seem to string together much more effortlessly.

A Daily Practice sustains us in a simple and practical way by keeping us rooted in who we are at our most elemental level. It removes the stress and agitation from our mind and body to allow our wiser unconscious to surface. Once it does, we have an unlimited source of support and sustenance.

At the foundation of a Daily Practice is self-love and compassion, which can prove to be the most difficult of all disciplines to adopt. Making time for yourself in the midst of daily demands and loving requests is a bold statement of commitment to your higher purpose in life and a reminder of that larger purpose as well. It is a key to your deeper intuitive wisdom, peace of mind, and ease of living.

Start your day with a Practice that sets a framework from which to build what you need to both support and energize. Care for yourself physically so that your larger objectives, so easily clouded by daily life, can come through. Every night, let go of that day to prepare for the next. Get ready to begin anew.

We can't step up into who we fully are with integrity until we address our basic needs. A Daily Practice needs to address the three cornerstones of Body, Mind, and Spirit. Practices such as yoga incorporate all three elements, but if you choose a Daily Practice that is sedentary, such as journaling, add in a physical element as well. Remembering *why* you practice (reconnecting to that deeper self, feeling the peace of mind, the calm) makes it easier to stay committed.

A Daily Practice doesn't, however, need to be done in a special room with fancy props or equipment. Any daily routine you are currently doing may work as a Practice if it helps you to clear away the excess of life and reconnect to your deeper self. Often, the bustle of daily life can hinder efforts to make a positive change in your life. This is what happened to Irene.

Irene was a newly retired widow who thought she would be able to dedicate her morning to a specific Daily Practice of yoga, meditation, and journaling. She had set aside space in her family room and bought a few special items to designate the area.

Major life events intervened just when the calm of a Daily Practice was needed most. She became the primary caretaker to her suddenly handicapped sister as well as the chief chauffeur and support to her young niece and nephew. Her sister's family practically lived with her, causing many sudden alterations in all of Irene's routines.

Because the Daily Practice concept was new to Irene, she didn't have a predetermined practice to fall back on or work from, so she abandoned the idea altogether and felt like she'd failed herself. We had been working together since her husband died several years earlier, and I asked her to describe her morning routine. She did the things many of us do: drank some water, made coffee or tea, showered, wrote her to-do list, and started her day.

These tasks were all just waiting to be turned into a Practice. I asked Irene if she could add a different intention to the activity, turning it into a deep connection to self and in the process transforming it into her Daily Practice. Irene was able to transform these simple tasks:

1. Drinking water, making coffee/tea became acts of mindfulness—simple, calming acts that she could habitually do in a meditative state while focusing on the present.

2. Showering was a visualization of washing away the old and bringing in the new, determining what the new day would deliver and stating how she would approach it.

3. In the margins of her to-do list, she wrote in some of her larger goals, an uplifting quote to keep her enthused, and an affirmation she wanted to remember throughout the day.

There are many reasons a Practice might not fit easily in one's day. It is important to find a method and a time that *do* work. Breaking the Practice into multiple sessions is just as beneficial.

Brad is a perfect example of a busy professional and a young parent who has little to no time for taking care of himself. He came to me to partner with him on his goals of starting a new business as a newly married man, raising a new family, and relocating to a different part of the country. Part of a loving, extended family, he had never been away from a ready source of support.

His days were full of entrepreneurial business meetings, employee hiring, charity, community functions, client networking, the nuts and bolts of a new business undertaking, the logistics of a personal move, caring for young children, and being an attentive husband. Being a dedicated man, he strove to exceed his expectations, which were much higher than anyone else had of him.

We worked together successfully on values and life purpose, but he insisted he had no extra time for a Daily Practice. However, once things slowed down, it would be the first thing he would do.

Within his day, what he did have without fail was driving time. I asked him to leave the house five or ten minutes earlier than usual for his commute. He said he could, and I suggested several options for him:

1. Listen to inspirational recordings while he drives.

2. Park the car in a quiet spot when he arrives five to ten minutes ahead of schedule, close his eyes, and visualize or meditate.

3. Park the car and walk for five to ten minutes.

I did insist that whichever option he chose, he was to consider it a Daily Practice and to do it every day, at the same time, if possible.

Brad, ever the overachiever, decided to do all three options. I met with him weekly, and the week after he had begun his Daily Practice, he reported that he was a convert to the Daily Practice "stuff." He enjoyed the inspirational recordings immensely and began amassing future ones so he wouldn't run out. He stopped taking calls in his car so that he could turn his full attention to the message.

The five to ten minutes of quiet time resulted in a quick catnap at first, but he even found that helpful, because when he awoke he was so refreshed that he felt inspired. After the third day, he was able to stay awake and found himself ruminating on the message in the recording he'd just finished. He built an extra five to ten minutes into every client appointment and took that time to walk. His mind creatively prepared for the meeting by allowing him to refocus on his best self.

You may find, as Brad did over time, that it is necessary to alter your Daily Practice occasionally to allow for changes in your routine or new constraints. Rather than give up your Daily Practice, change it to suit you, but continue practicing daily.

From nurturing yourself, a peace of mind and confidence grows that deepens and becomes a constant amid daily flux. It provides us with the key that unlocks the answers contained within us. It shows us where to look when the questions seem unfathomable. By developing this simple act, we commit to care for ourselves and experience more ease through life.

When we establish our Daily Practice, we are taking care of the cornerstones of Body, Mind, and Spirit. When one is out of balance, the other components in our life cannot continue working well indefinitely. This is as simple and as difficult as stopping the outside world momentarily and reflecting within ourselves; at some point, it becomes more difficult to go without this limitless support available to us than enduring the effort of going within. Our method of reflection is what differs among us—each of us can choose our portal of entry—Body, Mind, or Spirit.

EXERCISE ONE
DAILY PRACTICE

Here is a sample of Daily Practices that can be used as an isolated practice or in combination with one another. Remember to care for all components of yourself. If your daily habits include adequate physical self-care, make them part of your Daily Practice. The distinguishing factor of the Daily Practice is that it reconnects you to your deepest self.

Mindfulness. As a practice, mindfulness is intentional focus on the present, moment by moment, regardless of the activity. Observe your physical sensations, thoughts, and reactions as if witnessing them from a distance, without judgment. Then, release whatever is in that moment. Completely accept and let go allowing each given moment single minded focus.

Conscious breathing. As a Practice, conscious breathing involves regular, deep breathing. It serves as a meditation that can be done anywhere and is simultaneously calming and energizing. There are many specific breathing exercises, but to begin breathing as a Practice, take in one deep breath while counting the time it takes to fully inflate your lungs naturally. Slowly take the same number of counts to expel the breath. Repeat for as many minutes as you can dedicate to the practice.

Meditation. It isn't necessary to have a separate room, a meditation cushion or any other props to meditate. Begin by closing your eyes and allowing the external world to fade away with the exhalation of your breath. With the inhalation of your next breath, allow fresh insight and possibilities to enter. Repeat for as long as you have set aside for your Practice. When thoughts come to mind, allow them to come and just as easily go. Continue meditating until the time period is complete. For information on more advanced meditation techniques, or to develop your own style, go to chapter 7.

Visualization. One of the most effective ways to calm yourself in a visualization exercise is to picture yourself in the best possible outcome in the midst of your day. Surround yourself with helpful colleagues, friends, and supporters. Give yourself a phrase to motivate and empower you through the day and repeat it until you feel enthusiastically motivated. Refer to chapter 7 for additional visualization techniques.

Reading, contemplation, and reflection. As a Practice, contemplative reading, known as lectio divina, can help focus our thoughts and direct our actions to a positive result. Choose material that is meaningful, and select a short portion to read for the first part of the practice, followed with time for contemplation of what you've read. Then, take time to write down, or record in another manner, your reflections on the process.

Writing. Writing as a Practice is different than writing for a purpose. As a Practice, writing is the creative act of allowing whatever thoughts are present to come out; it allows the deeper self to communicate insights by surfacing new thoughts to record. Writing a set number of pages or for a set period of time per day is a way to use this practice.

Playing a musical instrument, painting, or other art form. When we use creativity as a Practice, it opens us to our deeper selves in the same way that writing does. It allows our busy conscious minds and bodies to actively create something while simultaneously asking the subconscious to come up with something new. We are literally inviting the creation to surface. And when the subconscious speaks, we are there ready to listen.

Active Practice of gratitude. Gratitude can be both an attitude and a Practice. Adopting both is a fabulous idea! As a practice, it is a daily discipline in which we note and list specifically what we are grateful for, even on the most dismal days. Having a set number of items to be grateful for is recommended. I suggest no less than ten per day. Write these down in a dedicated gratitude notebook.

Prayer. It doesn't matter what your religious beliefs are or are not. Having a Practice in which you offer your actions up for a higher purpose in life can bring you peace of mind, confidence, reconnection to your deeper self, and simultaneous calm and enthusiasm. Start by saying your own wishes, thoughts, and dreams and offering them up, or read a prayer book if that suits you.

Journal writing. As a Practice, journal writing can vary and deepen through the years, which makes it a rewarding discipline in which to see your life changes and growth. At its base is the constant reassurance of processing the daily events and stresses that you privately explore there. Beyond that, though, are the discoveries that appear unexpectedly as your wiser self shows up. With daily reflection, you begin to know yourself as never before, and the journal can become a confidant to work through all aspects of life. Aspects of the discipline that are imperative are being honest and authentic when writing and allowing reflective time for new thoughts to enter from your subconscious. If you are a highly visual person, making your journal a visual and written representation can be especially powerful.

Exercise. Exercise of any form (yoga, Pilates, walking, running, dance, tai chi, and so on) can be a Practice connecting us with our deeper self when we intentionally set that as our purpose, as seen in the example of Irene above. When we deliberately bring our soul into our physical practice, we have changed exercise from toning our body to reconnecting our total self. This is done through breath, thought, specific movement, and repetition. As the body and muscles relax, the subconscious mind surfaces, and the two begin working together. You will recognize this through experiences of creative insight and inspiration or sudden thought clarity and idea breakthroughs. Alternately, you can bring a specific prayer, positive intention, or thought to mind while exercising.

All the practices listed will work...if you do them. Decide to commit to a Daily Practice, and within three weeks you *will* experience a greater sense of personal presence and more clarity in your life. In the course of a year, your life will change.

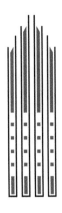

chapter five

Form a Structure
of Tactics

The mind's first step to self-awareness must be through
the body... First and foremost, be a good animal.

—GEORGE A. SHEEHAN

With your Daily Practice established as the foundation of your three-part Personal Template, you can now focus on developing a Structure of Tactics to confidently, comfortably, and joyfully live your purpose every day.

By the end of this chapter, you will know how to use a customized set of habits you intentionally form to respond to particular needs you have, to set yourself up for daily success, and to reinforce positive daily action.

Once you're clear on your values and your purpose, establishing Tactics to function at your optimum is easier because you have a concrete reason to do so. It becomes more than an abstract goal of eating healthy food to look and feel good or exercising to keep fit. These Tactics become the means to better understanding yourself and living your life mission. Tactics are simple routines that support your purpose. However, an unbalanced life can hinder your life purpose, as it did for my client Mark.

Mark illustrates how when life becomes disproportionate it affects life purpose and mission. He is a physician, so it isn't surprising to learn that his life purpose is to heal. His vision was working with adolescent boys gravely injured in team sports accidents. His mission was to rewrite local community team sport standards in concert with the local schools.

His patients and the community held Mark and his work in the highest esteem. He was in demand for social and professional events—for his expertise and because he was a warm, approachable, and humorous man. Unfortunately, he was also significantly overweight and functioned on six hours sleep per night and convenience food meals. At 52 years old, his body was tired in every way—taxed to function beyond its optimal limits.

Mark's turning point came when he was offered an opportunity to present his work to a national council of sports medicine. He would be required to travel weekly for a minimum period of six months to interact with a special cross-functional board. Following that, he would have speeches and presentations cross-country requiring monthly travel.

It was everything he'd worked for, wanted, and lived for. He knew he wasn't up for the task physically. He needed to make some personal changes to his Structure of Tactics. Simple, daily steps added up to major results and allowed him to live his purpose and his mission—and fulfill his vision. He began walking every morning at the school track, gradually increasing his distance. His food choices changed from convenience to a diet of basic, healthy three meals a day with small snacks that suited his body's needs. Before bedtime, he did some stretching exercises, and he was sure to get seven to eight hours of sleep.

It didn't take long for him to see changes and for his energy to increase. The rest of his life was already functioning well. Now he could enjoy full alignment.

Let's look at what would be useful to build as new layers to your Tactics. Evaluate your current habits and consider whether a new approach or a fresh intention could revitalize them to make them meaningful and help you accomplish the outcome you need. Craft this until your Tactics become the most rewarding part of your day.

Each cornerstone offers another way for us to understand ourselves. There is an interdependency between the components, so taking care of one neglected part will have benefits far beyond what we immediately apply. As you saw from Mark's example, taking care of his neglected physical needs allowed him to realize his life vision.

You may not need to establish an entirely new set of Tactics. Much like your Daily Practice, be aware that routines are already a big part of your everyday life. I encourage you to take control of your routines so that they are directing you where you want to go. How detailed and organized your Tactics become is completely up to you. Here's an exercise to help you determine whether you thrive on more organization or less. Once you are able to determine the style of routine that best suits you, we will go to the next step of creating the Structure of Tactics.

EXERCISE ONE
DESIGNING STRUCTURED ROUTINES

Answer the following questions:

1. Do you need more structure in your life overall?

2. Would you enjoy having more segmented blocks of time in your day?

3. Do you like to anticipate having the same activity each day at the same time?

If you answered yes to the above questions, you would benefit most from a structured routine at the beginning and end of each day. As you continue through this chapter and choose your activities, begin to put them into an order within specific blocks of time.

For those who enjoy structure, it can provide a sense of control and organization. For someone who prefers a freer approach to their day, too much structure can cause shallow breathing and anxiety! Consider which approach will best benefit you.

A structured routine will also provide specific blocks of time in which you will have specific activities to accomplish. Doing them will add to the sense of goal accomplishment. Not doing the prescribed activities may lead to an overall sense of disappointment, though. So, again, be aware of what motivates you. If you are motivated by an end objective, particularly one that is measurable in small, specific steps, go for the structure. If you are motivated by the overall journey and process, a rigid time frame isn't mandatory.

If you didn't answer affirmatively to the above questions, consider your answers to the exercise below so that we can fill in the details of your Structure of Tactics.

EXERCISE TWO
DESIGNING CREATIVE ROUTINES

Answer the following questions:

1. What gives me peace of mind?

2. How do I regain my energy, both mental and physical?

3. When do I have the most physical energy to accomplish tasks?

Our objective is to create activities to align ourselves to our purpose. For this process to be effective, it needs to be very personalized. Sitting and looking at a blue wall may be a valuable meditation for one person while for another it is painful emotionally, spiritually, and physically. The difference lies in the intention for the activity and also in the style of the individual. Take the time to craft your hours and days to suit you.

Len is a great example of someone who made creative use of a generous amount of unstructured time in meeting his responsibilities. As you will see, he also built in quite a few rituals within his unstructured time.

He was a carpenter who built fine wood designs for custom homes. His work required him to be both practical and creative, skills that he possessed in abundance. He worked in his workshop or at a home site every afternoon from 1:00 until 7:00 p.m. In the morning, however, he felt best leaving his time mostly open.

He did have a regular routine of waking up by 8:00 a.m., making coffee, and then running through a martial arts workout, but after that, he allowed unscheduled time to daydream, sketch, walk, read—or do whatever he cared to do. Without this time, he became anxious and irritable. It was his time for creative input, which allowed him to both conceive of his ideas and put to rest the ones he'd completed.

Every month or two he would become bored by whatever routines he'd established in his mornings and he'd change them. For the next period of time, he'd find himself at the market every morning or browsing the hardware store. But the constant of open time to fill as he chose remained. His parameters were his waking routine, his freedom of open time to fill creatively, his work hours, and his set evening time. During the evening he socialized in some way with others, having been alone the remainder of the day.

Total lack of established routines can cause a lack of focus and direction. Time can be wasted on meaningless activities rather than focused on more intentional efforts that can support your purpose, mission, and vision. This happened to Barbara. At 71 years of age, Barbara was free to fill in her days as she pleased and kept busy, but she wasn't satisfied with how she felt come the end of each day. Overall, she was dissatisfied with life.

We were working together on her life purpose and how her mission fit into the world post-retirement. I asked her to take a week to consider what gave her joy and instilled passion. She didn't have any difficulty answering. Her passions were gardening, cooking, and photography, and she took each of them to an art form. Since her retirement, she'd spent many hours filling her days with these activities, but what she lacked was routine and structure.

Barbara set a simple but distinct structure to her day. She decided to carve out her day into sections and establish set morning and evening routines, with the middle section of the day devoted to one of her three passions.

After following this new approach for one week, Barbara reported to me that she felt much more peace of mind as well as motivated to do her tasks for the day. After one month, it was impressive to see how much additional accomplishment she'd made in each of her favorite areas.

Before we look at how to build out the details of our Structure of Tactics, let's discuss some general elements of life to incorporate. You've seen in the example above how Barbara incorporated creativity within her Structure.

ALWAYS INCORPORATE JOY

Joy and laughter are an underdeveloped yet elemental part of life—and our birthright. How can you choose joy in your life? Living with joy assists you in accomplishing your objectives in living your life purpose. Now, determine what gives you joy in building your Structure, and include those elements regularly.

USE YOUR CREATIVITY

Perhaps Martha Graham expressed the importance of creativity best when she said, "There is a vitality, a life force, an energy, a quickening that is translated through you into action, and because there is only one of you in all time, this expression is unique. And if you block it, it will never exist through any other medium and will be lost." When you use others' creations, you lose one more opportunity to express your individual self in this world, and you miss out on the benefit of greater inspiration and encouragement.

We all have the ability to create something with our lives. It is up to us to decide what to create. It can be a tangible, artistic object such as a sculpture or painting, a book, a choreographed dance, or a film, or we can create a meaningful home, a family, a business, or a safe harbor for endangered animals or children. The options are endless.

It *can* feel like a formidable task because the fear we can feel as we fight is the resistance within ourselves to fully show who we are. Once we overcome that, we are more completely living our values and our purpose.

You reveal yourself through your creativity. When you decide to express yourself, you literally blaze through closed neurons in the brain. The style in which you create is what connects you to your greatest self. What we create is a calling that we alone hear from within. It is our fulfillment of our soul's deepest desire and can bring us great joy. Use the opportunity as you craft your day to fit in expressions of your unique creativity.

Imagination is what shows you how you will fulfill your life purpose. It opens a door between the subconscious and the mundane, taking inspiration and translating it to paper, canvas, stage, or daily life. Apply your skills, intelligence, and talents, and then allow imagination to run.

Practice creativity in every aspect of your day. Creating from a place of internal alignment puts you in a zone where time fades away. You are simultaneously part of something greater than yourself and detached from everything, in a place where you get a glimpse of the deep potential waiting. In this way, you show your purpose through your daily actions branded uniquely by you.

We require a sense of safety to live courageously, to be willing to stand up for our dreams and live our values confidently. We need to have the ability to open up to others comfortably while retaining our integral self. By establishing your Structure of Tactics, you are building out the details of your three-part Personal Template and establishing methods and techniques to establish a feeling of safety and maintain alignment.

The exercise below will help you begin organizing your Structure of Tactics. Consider the three cornerstones of Body, Mind, and Spirit in order to fine-tune the Tactics most suited to your current needs.

Remember, if you would find it easier or more convenient to download a workbook of Exercises, I've made these resources available for you at www.ItsNotThatComplicatedToolKit.com.

EXERCISE THREE
DETERMINE YOUR STRUCTURE OF TACTICS

The following list contains thought starters categorized for your exploration and organization. For each category, contemplate whether you feel a need to improve your current efforts in that area. Don't take the easy road out. If you know you would benefit from improving a specific cornerstone, now's the time.

For now, use the following information to choose which areas on which you'd like to focus. Activities for each will follow in Exercise 4. Jot down any thoughts that appeal to you and any that occur to you as you read.

1. BODY

- Take care of your body: This means sleep, exercise, nutrition, and as many health supplements you wish to add. The non-negotiables here, though, are sleep, exercise, and healthy nutrition.

- Grooming: Sure, it might sound basic, but isn't grooming a statement that we are valuing ourselves above other priorities in our life? When the phone rings or the kids are screaming and we choose to honor our dental appointment, isn't that a powerful message delivered simply that we take care of ourselves?

- Choose to breathe: Breath fully, calmly, and deeply. When you feel overwhelmed, it will focus you. At times of focus, it will energize you further. Breathing allows you to pause as you fill your lungs and enjoy the moment you are living.

- Manufacture a "perfect" environment: Fabricate a personal atmosphere that is ideal for your personal needs. It has been said many times, but it's your life. Live it your way, in your style. What would make it perfect for you? Organize it, beautify it, change it.

2. MIND

- Speak your truth: Is there something you are yearning to express that hasn't been said? Can it be done through an action? Living in integrity requires consistency between thoughts, words, and actions. Speaking our truth allows us to live in peace as it releases all possibility of regret.

- Make room in your head for your loved ones: Consider who is taking emotional space in your thoughts and whether they deserve it. If they enhance your life, and you enrich theirs, the answer is obvious. If not, why give them real estate in your head?

- Exercise your brain: There are countless ways to keep your brain healthy—everything from reading regularly, learning a musical instrument, doing puzzles, to doing specific brain exercises.

- Eliminate negativity: Fill your life with the messages and images that you want to live with. Populate it with the people you enjoy, books you want to read, movies and images you want to see, habits that reinforce you, and thoughts that inspire you.

- Establish healthy boundaries with others: Don't waste your energy making everyone else happy at your expense. Be responsible for your emotions and know that others have theirs, but you aren't responsible for them. Identify what you will accept, and say "no" to what you won't. Follow through on your decisions. Allowing others to act at your expense is a way of devaluing yourself. Be confident, and believe that you do matter—just as much as everyone else.

- Make healthy social connections: Make time for friends and loved ones. Spend time together doing things you mutually enjoy.

3. SPIRIT

- Consider this category the part of life that is larger than you, extending beyond this world. Whatever name you assign to it, consider the following:

- Meditating, mindfulness, or solitude: If your Daily Practice doesn't include any of these, I strongly encourage you to build at least one of them into your Structure of Tactics. This can be a matter of sitting alone quietly with your eyes gazing at your favorite object. The point is to relax the conscious mind so that the subconscious can surface.

- Practice of gratitude: The active practice of gratitude is essential for a fully aligned life. If gratitude isn't a component of your Daily Practice, consider adding it now to your Tactics. Truly appreciating and giving thanks for everything we have in life magnifies the opportunities we are given. By acknowledging what we are given, our eyes open to what is in front of us, allowing us to see even more opportunities and choose to accept them. Praise is a practice separate from gratitude and distinctly gives gratitude to a higher source for the blessings we receive.

- Forgive: Reflect on what is lodged hard in your heart, and work on letting it go. Even if you feel grievously harmed, forgiving will allow you to move forward. Forgiveness is something you do for yourself. The benefits of forgiving extend beyond the emotional release and to the physical benefit of lowered blood pressure, stronger immune system, and a drop in stress hormones, which have an impact on heart health. Besides, you will feel less anxiety and hostility and fewer symptoms of depression.[12]

- Be kind: Extend yourself to someone unexpectedly. Listen with your whole heart. Do the unasked favor just because you thought of it. Be a kind person who chooses actions according to your values.

- Write it down: Keep a dream journal or journal for inner exploration.

To fully function and thrive in our daily lives requires action after having established a firm foundation of self-confidence. Determining what is most important to us through our core values and then reinforcing everything in our lives around those values provides a blueprint that both guides and realigns us when we sway.

You create your Structure of Tactics to encourage and simplify your days. The objective is always to return to self-confidence through self-acceptance and compassion. Incorporating simple actions that reinforce your core values will sustain and motivate you. Over time, it may even transform your life.

Before you lock in your choices, assess whether your world feels overwhelming. If it does, return to the basics of sleep, proper

---

12 Mayo Clinic research

nutrition, and exercise. To those three, add quiet time, perhaps even during a walk, run, bike ride, or cooking a healthy meal. By simplifying schedules to these basics, time opens up. New ideas can follow as the next step once you have a chance for basic replenishment.

Even though self-care is in the Body cornerstone, its results reach far beyond the physical. By intentionally deciding to place your needs at the forefront, you reinforce your value and declare yourself a priority and take specific steps to support your goals.

Self-care in this way incorporates self-compassion and requires your integrity about what you truly need and want—and then taking action to support that. The following example shows how rewarding self-care at its deepest level can be.

Gary was a well-regarded local politician, well known and liked due to his integrity, kindness, and thoughtfulness, as well as his meaningful contributions to the community. It appeared that all aspects of his life were running well. At 68, he was in good physical shape, healthy, and happily married, and he enjoyed many leisure activities with friends and family.

The missing piece in all this was in how Gary treated himself. He kept his word to others at his own expense. His generosity and kindness frequently penalized him through his time, energy, and personal finances. The cost to himself wasn't apparent until he retired, when he began to see how others took his kindness as acquiescence.

Reestablishing borders wasn't easy for Gary, and it wasn't a fast process. It required a systematic examination of his reaction to each situation he encountered and a reflection on what his values were and how he truly felt. From there, he determined how he could best stay true to himself, be kind, and be honest.

In the process, some people didn't see Gary in the way they were accustomed. But he gained a new level of respect and a new social circle that honored him for his generous heart. Gary was able to establish his personal boundaries while garnering heartfelt regard within his community.

Take some time to fill in the specific activities in your Structure of Tactics for each cornerstone. Each individual is unique, and so are the Tactics that we each need at different times. The following exercise provides some general ideas. The activities for each will vary according to your needs. For more information and links to other activities to augment your Structure of Tactics, see the Resources section at the end of the book.

EXERCISE FOUR
STRUCTURE OF TACTICS: CHOICES

In Exercise Three, you chose the focus areas of your Tactics. Now, make decisions below based on what you will realistically do daily or weekly to support you in your values, purpose, and the work that you do.

1. Body

   Think of the body both physically and metaphorically. The body sheds cells because it no longer has use for them. They die and slough off. This shedding is an act of regeneration. New, young, fresh cells take their place. Consider the body's process as a metaphor for a total rejuvenation. On a daily basis, what thoughts and actions do we need to let go of, and which ones need to grow? Determine your activities as you keep those thoughts and actions in mind.

ENVIRONMENT

SAMPLE ACTIONS

Make room, literally and figuratively

Clear the chaos

Create a ritual

Establish a daily act of beauty such as bringing in a fresh flower or setting your favorite mug on the table before breakfast

Clean something daily

Make the bed every morning

Simplify whatever needs it

As you focus and listen to your body's processes, you'll begin to notice the clues it sends regarding its needs. Physical signs are always an indication that some type of care is needed. They can be an early indicator of illness or disease and also of emotional distress. Even imbalanced eating provides clues as to what is out of balance, from a need for certain vitamins or nutrients to unexpressed emotions. Any way you look at it, our body is a phenomenal source of information.

The following chart lists various actions that can be built upon each other or chosen separately. Consider if you have pain or discomfort in any specific area. If you do, look up resources[13]

---

13 Inna Segal, *The Secret Language of Your Body: The Essential Guide to Health and Wellness.* (New York: Simon & Schuster, Inc., 2010)

to know where to specifically address your attention. In the same way, pay attention to your current eating habits to honestly self-assess where you feel out of balance. Take time to jot down any insights. Next, make your choice of actions to add from the chart below that will most positively support your current needs.

MOVEMENT	NUTRITION	SLEEP	PHYSICAL NURTURE
SAMPLE ACTIONS			
Choose your rhythm, pace, and location. Will you be indoors or outdoors, alone or with others, at home or at a studio or gym? Direct ALL the details and have fun!	No single diet works for everyone. Choose any of the details below that may be useful for your food plan. Refer to the simple guidelines that follow	Sleep is a restorative way to literally shed one day and wake to the new. Consider the following to create a bedtime ritual	What simultaneously soothes and nurtures you physically?
Engage in team sports—a neighborhood or community league, a basketball game, etc.	Plan weekly menus, organize shopping lists, and batch cook to simplify your week	Take a warm bath an hour before bed with Epsom salts. The magnesium in Epsom salts relaxes the muscles	Schedule body treatments: massages, skin therapies, exfoliations, wraps, soaks
Start a home-based exercise program: recordings, yoga, weights, etc.	Drink more water	Drink herbal tea containing chamomile, valerian root, passionflower, lemon balm and kava, or warm milk before bedtime	Grooming care: pedicures, facials, hair treatments, manicures, skin care, etc.

MOVEMENT	NUTRITION	SLEEP	PHYSICAL NURTURE

SAMPLE ACTIONS

MOVEMENT	NUTRITION	SLEEP	PHYSICAL NURTURE
Choose your rhythm, pace, and location. Will you be indoors or outdoors, alone or with others, at home or at a studio or gym? Direct ALL the details and have fun!	No single diet works for everyone. Choose any of the details below that may be useful for your food plan. Refer to the simple guidelines that follow	Sleep is a restorative way to literally shed one day and wake to the new. Consider the following to create a bedtime ritual	What simultaneously soothes and nurtures you physically?
Walk, run, or bike—alone or with a dog or companion	Set a beautiful table and prepare for your meal	Turn off all electronic devices, including TVs at least one hour before bedtime and begin winding down mentally with breathing or gentle stretching exercises. Blue light emitted from electronic emissions will disturb sleep patterns	Breathe

MOVEMENT	NUTRITION	SLEEP	PHYSICAL NURTURE
SAMPLE ACTIONS			
Choose your rhythm, pace, and location. Will you be indoors or outdoors, alone or with others, at home or at a studio or gym? Direct ALL the details and have fun!	No single diet works for everyone. Choose any of the details below that may be useful for your food plan. Refer to the simple guidelines that follow	Sleep is a restorative way to literally shed one day and wake to the new. Consider the following to create a bedtime ritual	What simultaneously soothes and nurtures you physically?
Take part in Dance, Tai Chi, Aikido, martial arts, weights, Pilates, etc.	Drink water with fruit or herbs (mint, basil) or tea as you cook your meal	Read a relaxing or inspirational book or listen to a recording	Organize your clothes or personal items

Tune into what your body is asking for from a nutritional standpoint. While there is no single diet that works for everyone, there are a few simple guidelines that are universal:

- Eat real food.

- Eat what your body needs and not too much. Eat if you're hungry, but don't force it.

- Enjoy nutritious food.

- Eat locally and seasonally when possible.

From this list, the options are up to you. Not everyone functions at their best as a vegan or a meat eater. You will only know by paying attention to your body's clues. Pay attention to how you feel after you eat, and eat what makes you feel good.

2. MIND

Consider which of the following activities might benefit your Structure in the Mind cornerstone if you need to strengthen this layer. The categories are organized to allow for your creative thought. Refer back to your original notes to see where your greatest needs are.

CONNECTIONS	CLARITY	EXPANSION
SAMPLE ACTIONS		
Strengthen your ability to speak your truth or enhance social connections	Eliminate negativity or establish healthy boundaries	Exercise your brain and encourage new ideas
Organize a party	Laugh	Learn a new language or a musical instrument
Talk or spend time with a friend	Watch or read something funny or inspirational	Enroll in a class
Play with animals or children	Make lists of your nonnegotiables in life, your goals, your dreams, etc.	Write a poem, story, play, movie, article, etc.
Play a game, do a puzzle, etc.	Write a letter.	Plan a trip
Create a website or start a blog	Write in your journal	Explore a new hobby
Join a theatre or other community group	Imagine your best self in five years and your life then. Determine who and what you need in your world to create and sustain that reality	Read a different genre book

CONNECTIONS	CLARITY	EXPANSION
SAMPLE ACTIONS		
Strengthen your ability to speak your truth or enhance social connections	Eliminate negativity or establish healthy boundaries	Exercise your brain and encourage new ideas
Volunteer	Write a list of 100 things you like about yourself	Do brain exercises
Join a public speaking forum	Use affirmations	Write your memoir
Use local shops and services	Imagine your perfect day, and then create the best possible version of it	Change your routine
Practice true listening in conversations	Have that difficult conversation that needs to be had	Use new vocabulary

3. SPIRIT

Consider the following chart of options as you decide how to address caretaking this cornerstone. What is lacking, and what is the natural rhythm that feels most comfortable to you to rejuvenate and inspire you?

CORNERSTONE OF SPIRIT
SAMPLE ACTIONS
Spending time in nature
Breathing exercises
Receptive journal writing
Meditation
Mindfulness
Solitude

CORNERSTONE OF SPIRIT

SAMPLE ACTIONS

Practice of gratitude

Yoga or other physical movement as spiritual practice

Chakra alignment

Prayer, worship

Chanting

Reflective reading and contemplation (lectio divina)

Creativity

Dream work

Loving kindness

Our emotions impact our physical body—there is a distinct mind-body connection. As you've created your Structure of Tactics, consider how all the cornerstones communicate with each other. Just as your thoughts will affect how much energy you have to direct toward your to-do list that day, remember that your body is sending you information all day as well. Be sure you have addressed its communication as well as listened to the messages your subconscious is sending, which will lead you to greater accomplishments than you may be able to imagine at this time.

Now that the two portions of Daily Practice and Structure of Tactics in your Template are constructed, things should run smoothly most days. Your needs will change, which will cause your Daily Practice to also change. In the next chapter, we will see how adjustments are made when the unexpected happens.

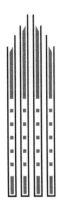

chapter six

Build a Bundle of Exceptional Resources

one day you finally knew

what you had to do, and began,

though the voices around you

kept shouting

their bad advice...

—MARY OLIVER, "THE JOURNEY"

The Bundle of Exceptional Resources is the third and final set of tools in your Personal Template toolkit. It is full of additional resources for comfort, for stretching yourself, and for taking you beyond the daily scope of your routines—all for the benefit of realigning yourself. By using the highly personalized tools in our Bundle during especially challenging times, we remain integrated with our values and in alignment with the ability to live joyfully. They are available when emergencies set in to help you acknowledge and work through difficult times—to regain alignment.

Alan enlisted my help to align the vision of his company with that of his Board of Directors. He was a focused man, well aware of the personal disciplines that were helpful in supporting his efforts. He had his Daily Practice established and Structure of Tactics functioning well.

Then one evening life threw him a curveball—his son killed a pedestrian in a car accident. This tragedy left him unable to make sense of his world. We began to look for the tools that would help him beyond what he was already using. Alan's Daily Practice and Structure were working very well, but they just weren't enough for his new circumstances.

Though our situations may not be as extreme as Alan's, we all need something extra when life feels out of control. There are a wealth of options to explore. Again, reflect on which of the cornerstones (Body, Mind, or Spirit) needs the most support and start looking for reinforcement tools there. Consider any of the tools you didn't use in your Daily Practice or Structure of Tactics as potential components of your Exceptional Resources Bundle. The next exercise will expand your thoughts for more ideas. *(Check the Resources for additional books and references.)*

Here's the part where you will either have a lot of fun exploring or be uncomfortable stretching your limits. Unusual times invite exploration, so stretch your comfort zone and ruminate on new possibilities. This is where the Exceptional Resources Bundle will come in, something that handles the extra credit when you need it.

The Bundle doesn't replace the other components of our Template. The Bundle resources are additions rather than substitutions. As you look over the chart, you will see that some are supplementary actions (such as utilizing essential oils) while others are potentially one-time efforts.

The Bundle is perhaps the most personalized module of your Template. Whatever challenges you face in your psyche and along the path of life, your individual Bundle will have a response for it. Individual A, for example, may be a very intellectual, hard-driven individual that finds themselves plagued on occasion by anxiety and depression. Their Bundle may include essential oils, body therapies, and movement classes customized for them. These solutions work because they have been personally chosen for effect.

EXERCISE ONE
BUNDLE RESOURCES

Options for challenging times. Explore those of the following that pique your interest.

SAMPLE ACTIVITIES

BODY	MIND	SPIRIT
Learn and use Feng Shui in your home and life. Or hire a professional	Choose a daily, weekly, or monthly motto to organize and motivate your current life inspirational theme. Support it through pictures, quotes, etc.	During your meditation or quiet time, take time for two components: gratitude and request for what you would like to receive next
Set intentions for your home	Create a to-do list or memo pad with value, purpose, affirmation, reminders, quotes or mottoes on the page. If created virtually, these can easily be updated	Consider whether the science of astrology conveys information in a way that unlocks information for your subconscious. If so, study the patterns between astrological events and human interaction

BODY	MIND	SPIRIT
Reestablish your life in rhythm with nature and the seasons. Create rituals and routines by week, month, quarter, and year.	Create soundtracks. Build various ones for reflection, inspiration, energy, motivation, etc.	Use tarot or oracle cards as a means to unlock the subconscious mind.
Add living essences to your nutrition: herbs, spices, tea, flowers, etc.	Make a vision board	Add mudras to a meditation practice.
Add essential oils to your physical discipline.	Listen to Ted talks and other positive reinforcement for life purpose and motivation. Or read similar material.	Chakra alignment
Infrared sauna.	Service, community	Sound toning
Float or isolation tank	Use affirmations and mental imagery	Study of universal truths and wisdom or mystery schools
Acupressure	Reframe situations for a different understanding and a more positive outcome	Communication with angels
Acupuncture	Chunk down tasks and goals	Tibetan rites movement
Emotional Freedom Technique (EFT) or Tapping	Hobbies and leisure	Color therapy
Release work in fascia	Set daily intentions	Chanting
Singing	Construct a book or list of quotes from your favorite leaders, authors, artists, etc.	Walking labyrinth
Aikido, yoga, or any other movement as practice	Drawing	Add candles to meditation

BODY	MIND	SPIRIT
Consciously reduce stress	Aromatherapy	Prayer, worship, grace
Deliberately eliminate anxiety.	Write your life plan in detail. Depict it graphically creatively.	Chant mantras.
Rolfing or other manual manipulation	Practice positive reframing: look for the opportunity and gift in each situation.	Crystals, gemstones

Some tools overlap the cornerstones. *Integrating* these with our values allows us to assimilate them within us for total alignment. As we assimilate these methods, we simultaneously create neural pathways that generate physical hormones and chemicals to assist us in our life processes. What we do as a simple routine of breathing exercises in the morning becomes much more as it calms our mind, energizes our body, and generates inspiration, as it did for my client Lynn.

Lynn was a very private woman who had gone through many challenges in life. I met her after she'd overcome several of them and was struggling with a new occurrence of grief. At 61, she'd used each occurrence of grief to pay attention to the message within it and to take an opportunity from it. Without many people knowing her life story, she exuded a calm and confidence that drew others to her.

As we worked together, I discovered she already had established a Daily Practice. She woke very early and spent 20-30 minutes meditating and then writing in her journal. Her journal entries always included a list of at least ten things she was most grateful for. Although she didn't consider herself a religious person, she had a deep faith in a greater power and spent time throughout her day in prayer.

Her Structure of Tactics was also well formed. She walked her dogs daily and took a yoga class three times a week. She followed a seasonal calendar of self-nurturing care and looked forward to scheduling various appointments for acupuncture and body treatments.

Lynn's mind was razor sharp. She painted, sculpted, and made lists, filling notebook after notebook. So when she came to me with grief after her husband died, we had to dig deep for some special resources.

Comfortable with meditation, she began to contemplate what would be helpful and made new lists of ideas. She then spent one day per week in a drawing workshop in a nearby community. This had far-reaching effects. Not only did she meet new people, but she explored a new area and was introduced to new ideas. She became interested in gemstones and began sculpting with various gems and stones in clay. To remind her of this time, she sculpted a beautiful hummingbird representing strength, joy, and endurance as well as beauty.

Lynn has adjusted and no longer uses all the tools from her toolkit, though she does still follow the other components of her Template. Thankfully, that chapter ended but not without her feeling she benefited from it.

Much like life, there are a lot of choices and options for you to consider here. To simplify, here's an overview and another worksheet.

EXERCISE TWO
YOU

Complete the following information about yourself:

1. My values

2. My personal creed or philosophy of life

3. My life purpose

4. My life mission

5. My life vision

6. My current Daily Practice

7. My Structure of Tactics (regular routines that support me to be my best)

8. My Bundle of Exceptional Resources that gets me back on track

Are all areas of your life represented well? Consider the Wheel of Life once again, on page 53.

Remember, your Personal Template is a lifelong power kit for alignment, serving to help you move forward but also to realign and refocus as needed and to integrate all areas of your life. The Template is never frozen or static. It evolves as your needs change.

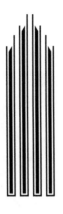

part three

SYNTHESIS

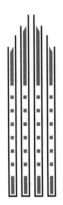

chapter seven

Information Is Everywhere: Receiving Answers

Learning is the beginning of wealth. Learning is the beginning of health. Learning is the beginning of spirituality. Searching and learning is where the miracle process all begins.

—JIM ROHN

The world is infused with potential guidance, in every corner of creation, for us to understand and interpret our life. We have endless opportunities to learn how to live our purpose, maintain alignment, and live joyfully.

You've learned that one aspect of fully moving into your life purpose is the ability to develop alignment. When you understand your values and your purpose and put your Personal Template together, you have everything you need to conquer any hurdles you may encounter. It's time to embrace full self-acceptance and appreciate your abilities. Listening to the signs along the way is *how* you can confidently claim your mission and embrace your vision.

Your greatest resource in this search for total self-acceptance is you. The human body is a comprehensive storehouse of intelligence, retaining knowledge in every cell and system. The human brain, heart, body, and spirit as we understand it is operating at only a fraction of its full potential despite the advances we have seen in our lifetime. I believe we all have within us the potential for tremendous feats—coming together as superhuman, superpower nations that are, in reality, entirely human and normal.

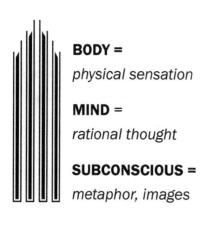

BODY =
physical sensation

MIND =
rational thought

SUBCONSCIOUS =
metaphor, images

Decoding the knowledge we do possess requires learning how to hear and translate the information that is within the cornerstones of Body, Mind, and Spirit.

Each of the cornerstones has its own language and communication style. Each sends us information constantly, often duplicating messages so that we have many opportunities to listen.

Regardless of where it occurs, any disharmony residing in one area compromises progress. Body, Mind, and Spirit are linked in an intrinsic pattern of feedback. You are given information in at least one of the three portals (and often more than one) to assist you in gaining traction in your life direction. For example, if you are rigidly grasping onto an idea, insisting on clenching to one fixed opinion, that inflexibility can prevent you from seeing problem-solving alternatives. We can get in our own way.

Let's look at each of the cornerstones and what they are trying to tell us.

SYMPTOMS OF SPINAL MISALIGNMENT

AREAS CONTROLLED BY NERVES	POSSIBLE EFFECTS OF A MALFUNCTION
NECK REGION	
Blood supply to the head, pituitary gland, scalp, bones of the face, brain, inner ear, middle ear, outer ear, sympathetic nervous system, eyes, optic nerves, auditory nerves, sinus, mastoid bones, tongue, forehead, cheeks, teeth, trifacial nerve, nose, lips, mouth, eustachian tube, vocal cords, neck glands, pharynx, neck muscles, shoulders, tonsils, thyroid gland, bursae in the shoulders, elbows.	Headaches, nervousness, insomnia, head colds, high blood pressure, migraine headaches, nervous break-downs, amnesia, chronic tiredness, dizziness, sinus trouble, allergies, crossed eyes, deafness, eye troubles, earache, fainting spells, vision dif-ficulties, neuralgia, neuritis, acne or pimples, eczema, hay fever, hearing loss, adenoids, laryngitis, hoarseness, sore throats, quincy, stiff neck, pain in upper arm, tonsillitis, whooping cough, croup, bursitis, colds, thyroid conditions.
MID-BACK	
Arms form the elbows down (including hands, wrists and fingers), esophagus, trachea, heart (including valves and covering), coronary arteries, lungs, bronchial tubes, pleura, chest, breast, gall bladder, common duct, liver, solar plexus, blood, stomach, pancreas, duodenum, spleen, adrenal and supra-renal glands, kidneys, ureters, small intestines, lymph circulation.	Asthma, cough, difficult breathing, shortness of breath, pain in lower arm, pain in hands, functional heart condi-tions, chest conditions, bronchitis, pleurisy, pneumonia, congestion, influenza, gall bladder condition, jaundice, shingles, liver conditions, fevers, low blood pressure, anemia, poor circulation, arthritis, stomach troubles, nervous stomach, indigestion, heartburn, dyspepsia, ulcers, gastritis, low resistance to colds and disease, allergies, hives, kidney troubles, hardening of the arteries, chronic tiredness, nephritis, pyelitis, acne, pimples, eczema, boils, rheumatism, gas pains, sterility.
LOW BACK	
Large intestines, inguinal rings, appendix, abdomen, upper leg, sex organs, uterus, bladder, knees, prostate gland, muscles of the lower back, sciatic nerve, lower legs, ankles, feet.	Constipation, colitis, dysentery, diarrhea, ruptures, hernias, cramps, difficult breathing, acidosis, varicose veins, bladder troubles, menstrual troubles such as painful or irregular periods, miscarriages, bed wetting, impotency, change of life symptoms, knee pains, sciatica, lumbago, difficult, painful or too frequent urination, backaches, poor circulation in the legs, swollen ankles, weak ankles and arches, cold feet, weakness in the legs, leg cramps.
PELVIS	
Hip bones, buttocks, rectum, anus.	Low back pain, spinal curvature, hemorrhoids (piles), pruritis (itching), pain at the end of spine on sitting.

Cervical Spine

1st Thoracic

Thoracic Spine

1st Lumbar

Lumbar Spine

Sacrum

Coccyx

THE BODY

The body communicates with us through *sensation*. You've hopefully experienced optimal physical performance when everything is going well. In contrast, when something is out of order, your body will signal it with a sign of discomfort, pain, or injury. You may first detect it in a change of **breath pattern** and then as **discomfort in part of your body**. Finally, pain settles into an injury or **scar tissue**.

Taking responsibility for living your purpose means being accountable for whatever condition your body is in and guiding it to the best outcome. Your body is a physical tool that allows you to act in life and needs to be handled with more regard than you would give any other possession. Tune into your body's signals to hear if you are currently giving it the best treatment possible.

The exercise below will allow you to tune into the most accessible feedback mechanism you have: your breath. Watch where you may be holding your breath as you inhale and exhale.

EXERCISE ONE
BREATHING

You are usually aware if you are holding tension in your body, but it is possible to adapt to a level of persistent tension that becomes a new normal. To test your current level of tension, take a deep breath and do a body scan. If you are strained, you won't physically be able to breathe freely and deeply. Your diaphragm simply will not inflate and function correctly, and it will not be able to connect with the organs and systems within your physiology.

Check these three areas of your body in particular for tension and consider what they could indicate to you.

1. Are your hands or fingers gripped tight?

2. Is your jaw clenched? Are you gritting your teeth?

3. Are your hips tight? Are you able to walk easily, loosely, and freely? When you get up and down, can you move smoothly?

If you found any of these parts of your body tight, clench them even tighter for ten seconds, then relax and stretch them. Extend the body part. If your hips are tight, unclench and loosen the muscle connection from the thigh to the hip. Imagine each component of your body as separate but connected, operating cooperatively and independently.

You can do this exercise throughout the day, even when driving. It is both relaxing and informative as well as useful for resetting your current stress level.

Proper breathing allows one trillion neuro-connections, permitting oxygen saturation and neurological organization within your cells.[14] If you are holding on to pressure, as you have seen, it is impossible to completely release, relax, and breathe. Simply making a commitment to breathe deeply and regularly will help release and heal your body and aide you in moving forward.

---

14 Lois Laynee, *Laynee Restorative Breathing Method,*
http://restoringbreathing.com/laynee-breathing-method/

Pain or discomfort is an obstacle that needs to be handled before you can advance aggressively in your life plans. Your body doesn't distinguish between physical and psychological trauma. If you are suffering to any degree, get to the source and resolve it. The problem-solving process will itself be enlightening, as it promotes further action and affects how you proceed. Taking action creates and maintains alignment and reinforces your purpose.

Consider whether you have pain in your body now and what it might connote. For the exercise below, conduct another body scan, this time paying attention to all sensations within the muscles and physical components of your body.

EXERCISE TWO
PHYSICAL SCAN

You may want to have your notebook close by as you observe where you have pain or discomfort. While some areas are most likely well known to you, some of the subtleties may surprise you. Jotting these areas down will be useful in setting up plans to resolve them later.

Sit quietly and pay attention to how your body feels with all aches and pains, stiffness, and tightness. Staying relaxed, picture a pen-sized laser slowly scanning your body inch by inch, head to toe. Make a note of every area where you feel tension, pain, or discomfort.

Now, refer to the charts "The Emotional Energy Centers of the Body" on page 67 and "Symptoms of Spinal Misalignment" on page 117. These illustrate a few of the ways your body reflects discordance. Consider what may be applicable for you, and make a note for yourself. Take as much time as you need for this and return to it until you feel you have some answers regarding the root cause of your pain. Inna Segal's book, *The Secret Language of Your Body*, gives a comprehensive overview of potential translations between mind and body sensations, organized from both an emotional and a physical perspective. For example, addiction to smoking can have its foundation in an emotional connection to a family member. Once that connection is handled more appropriately, a healthier habit can be formed.[15] Tuning into the messages your body sends you can be a valuable, practical tool from which you can even gain business results.[16] From your personal deductions, you can begin to craft an action plan that is appropriate for you.

The more observant and aware you are, the more you will be able to figure out what different symptoms indicate. The human body suffers the same—we all have headaches, stomachaches, and so on, but what those aches and pains represent to you can differ from the meaning they have for someone else. So it is critical that you take the time and regard to decipher this for yourself. Your migraine may be a signal that once again, you have relinquished your personal power—providing you with a monitor to reassess and act more appropriately next time. My sore throat might be my cue to release anger I harbor over an old grudge and to speak up to get over the paralyzing pain.

---

15 Inna Segal, *The Secret Language of Your Body: The Essential Guide to Health and Wellness* (New York: Simon & Schuster, 2010), Introduction.

16 ibid.

Fascia is interwoven tissue in our body that surrounds and interpenetrates every muscle, bone, nerve, artery, and vein, as well as our organs.[17] Research is continuing to uncover more data about this connective tissue, but what is already known is very helpful for identifying blockages in the body, including adhesions and scars, and for releasing them. The fascia is where we store all our pain[18] and therefore is also where we can release it.

There is always a message, a lesson, a gift, and an opportunity presented to us in these symptoms. The extent of information can be overwhelming and make it difficult to know where to look for answers. If you listen to what is either talking the loudest—often through pain—or whispering the most fervently, you won't miss the message or the opportunity to yield to the pressure in order to release it.

EXERCISE THREE
PHYSICAL ADHESIONS

Lay with your back on the floor, and using a small ball such as a tennis or lacrosse ball, put it gently at the base of your skull. Slowly move it around your head and neck, turning in all directions, noticing where there are distinct places where your body moves less fluidly, almost as if it is stuck. This will feel like a knot or a jammed place—a sensation deeper and more significant than the tenderness of a sore muscle.

---

17 Thomas W. Myers, *Anatomy Trains: Myofascial Meridians for Manual and Movement Therapists* (London: Churchill Livingstone, Third Edition, 2014).

18 John F. Barnes, *Myofascial Release: The Search for Excellence* (Pennsylvania: Rehabilitation Services, Inc., 1990).

Continue down your back, shoulders, sides, hips, and legs. Turn on your side and perform the same exercise on your sides and the other angles of your legs and arms.

Make notes in your notebook where any restrictions were found. Reflect on whether you had surgeries at any time in that area or experienced an illness, ongoing anxiety, or stress that manifested in physical symptoms there. Take as much time as needed to gain the insights you need before moving on to a resolution, which is to release any physical pain in your body in order to achieve alignment.

There are many methods for releasing physical pain, including acupuncture, acupressure, yoga, and Pilates, thereby allowing further movement. Physical pain can thwart any progress you make toward your life purpose, but releasing it, like Drake did, will assist you in aligning with your purpose.

Drake became my client when he decided to combine his success as a professional runner and business. He wasn't sure how to put it all together, but he somehow knew it was part of his life purpose to work with other runners, leveraging his past success to help them.

We worked through the components of clarifying his values, and he defined his life purpose, articulated his mission, and explored his vision. He was already well versed in a Daily Practice of meditation and running and had a Structure of Tactics that supported him. He moved quickly through several weeks of progress, enthusiastically accomplishing everything he set out to do.

At week six of our work together, everything stopped. Drake came in for a session discouraged and physically limping. He told me he had a muscle injury in his psoas muscle and wasn't able to get beyond it.

He was willing to use it as an opportunity to explore a different level of information. The psoas is a deep muscle that runs from the spine to the femur and is difficult to stretch and release through daily activity. Fascia envelops it, and adhesions can cause it to bind up and tighten even further.

Drake was amenable to work with a trained Pilates instructor and enrolled in a program that incorporated release work of the psoas, specific stretching and strengthening movement, and careful posture alignment both in and out of class. As he did, he moved through his physical blockage and through body scans to discover some fears regarding his public persona and his new business. He had been known as a runner, not a businessperson.

He worked through these fears by continuing his movement practice and also by handling his thoughts individually, considering whether they had merit or were just fears in taking the next step in life. To his surprise, he found himself experiencing more creativity around putting his business together.

Release work is important, and it's easy to incorporate into your Personal Template once you calculate what method works best for your needs. As Drake did, you will often see results far beyond the physical relief from pain. However, just like Drake, you may also encounter problems like fear, which will reveal itself through tense muscles, headaches, and so on.

Problems occur when you don't pay attention. Paying attention alerts us to patterns. For example, a tense jaw or nervous stomach alerts you to a physical imbalance. If you've taken care of the jaw or stomach at the time you realized it, tension was released, and you were able to move on. Your body, at the same time, was able to continue progressing with its functioning, optimizing cell function, nutrition, and all the myriad tasks it repetitively performs. If, however, you didn't stop to release that tension and it gets built up, after a long habit of repetitive pattern, pain will get trapped in the fascia, adhesions will build, and, in the case of injuries, scar tissue will form.

Scar tissue and adhesions build up in the connective tissue to protect the body as it heals. Once an area is healed, that excess tissue can be released. If allowed to remain, excess scarring and adhesions can cause stress on surrounding muscles and joints; compress nerves, blood vessels, and organs; and restrict physical and physiological movement.

Some specific ways to break up adhesions within your fascia are deep tissue massages, Active Release Techniques (ART—a specific style of deep tissue massage), specific yoga and Pilates movement disciplines focusing on appropriately working the fascia and not just stretching the muscles, and release work through rolling and pressure points.

MIND: THOUGHTS AND EMOTIONS

The rational mind uses the operating system of the brain, which allows you to function in the everyday world. It relates with logic and vocabulary and communicates in rational thought patterns. Emotions are the psychological component and are expressed in subjective feelings, experienced both physically and mentally. For example, fear is a specific emotion with psychological and emotional reactions, such as the psychological reaction of refusing to climb a ten-foot ladder while your body's physical response sends your heart racing. Emotions are another way that you receive signals, alerting you to your needs. Because they are a reaction to a situation, you have control over them. If ignored, your subconscious will find another way to get the message through to you until you respond.

Our nervous system is interconnected with our musculoskeletal system. When we experience strong emotions, four parts of the physical brain intersect: the limbic system, which regulates instinct, intuition, and emotions; the hypothalamus master gland, connected to the endocrine and digestive systems; the amygdala, which stores memory, motivation, and learning; and the cortex, which regulates thoughts.[19] This complex cranial operation makes traces on your body as you think and experience emotions.

Every thought and feeling you have triggers the release of neuropeptides, brain chemicals that control certain functions of your body. "The body mind can repress emotions and behavior. It uses neuropeptides in this process, substances that influence mood."[20] Neuropeptides are responsible for thousands of unique functions and include endorphins, adrenaline, oxytocin, and cortisol, which alert us to pleasure, pain, stress, and many other conditions. You can approach release work either through the emotions or through the physical pain, if that is what is more dominant. Refer to the "Emotional Pain Chart" on the following page for reference.

Sam did exactly that—he wanted to change his business model. He was confident and clear with his life purpose of bringing people from various walks of life together to help others. He'd been fulfilling his purpose via his mission of an environmental safety business he established, but he felt the need for a change.

---

19 Vicky Vlachonis, *The Body Doesn't Lie: A 3-Step Program to End Chronic Pain and Become Positively Radiant* (HarperOne, 2014).

20 Candace B. Pert, *Molecules of Emotion: The Science Behind Mind-Body Medicine* (Scribner, 2010).

This restlessness was a trademark of Sam's. Periodically, he would become unable to carry out his work due to some physical ailment or extreme emotional distress. He'd undergone extensive therapy throughout his life and had a thorough understanding that many of his behaviors were the result of an abusive childhood. Yet he continued to show physical remnants that affected his daily life.

Happily married and settled as a successful business owner, he was able to accommodate his needs, but he was no longer willing to put up with the discomfort and inconvenience. He was also very disappointed at having missed some fabulous opportunities due to feeling poorly in the past.

Since he'd already dealt with his issues through therapy, I suggested he work with therapeutic methods that would physically release trauma before we reviewed what a revised mission might look like. Sam began with deep tissue massage, followed at home with Epsom salt baths. He also initiated a practice of releasing through rolling and pressure points before daily breathing and yoga movement. He also visited an acupuncturist weekly.

In the first week of treatments, Sam felt physical release from so many different places that he was unable to distinguish it. The second week, he felt calmer, and by the end of the month, he was processing his emotions and thoughts with the absence of physical discomfort.

He incorporated his release work, breathing, and yoga as part of his Structure of Tactics after three months of working with professionals and intensive help. Today he has expanded his business model. Sam still has his environmental safety company, but today his mission includes managing an inner city center where business leaders act as informal mentors to young boys and girls. In the last nine months, Sam hasn't missed a day due to ill health, either physical or emotional.

EMOTIONAL PAIN CHART
THOUGHT PATTERNS THAT CONNECT WITH OUR EXPERIENCES

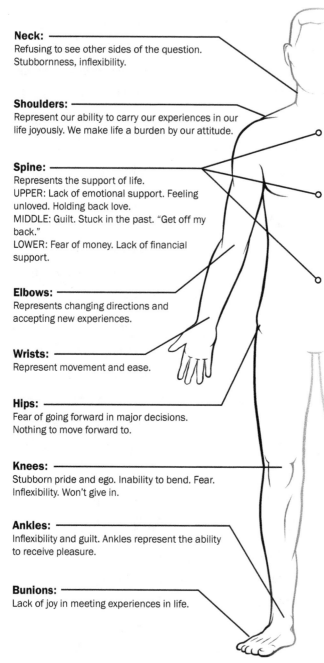

Neck:
Refusing to see other sides of the question.
Stubbornness, inflexibility.

Shoulders:
Represent our ability to carry our experiences in our
life joyously. We make life a burden by our attitude.

Spine:
Represents the support of life.
UPPER: Lack of emotional support. Feeling
unloved. Holding back love.
MIDDLE: Guilt. Stuck in the past. "Get off my
back."
LOWER: Fear of money. Lack of financial
support.

Elbows:
Represents changing directions and
accepting new experiences.

Wrists:
Represent movement and ease.

Hips:
Fear of going forward in major decisions.
Nothing to move forward to.

Knees:
Stubborn pride and ego. Inability to bend. Fear.
Inflexibility. Won't give in.

Ankles:
Inflexibility and guilt. Ankles represent the ability
to receive pleasure.

Bunions:
Lack of joy in meeting experiences in life.

How It Works:
Our body movement is reflective of our inner world. Align your
body, strive to be pain-free. Be
conscious in your body while
instinctively bringing awareness
to your life. A clearer mind helps
you to expend energy towards a
life you love.

Other Connections:
Arthritis: Feeling unloved.
Criticism. Resentment.
Bone Breaks/Fractures:
Rebelling against authority.
Bursitis: Repressed anger.
Inflammation: Fear. Seeing red.
Inflamed thinking.
Joint Pain: Represent changes in
direction in life and the ease of
these movements.
Loss of Balance: Not centered.
Scattered thinking.
Sciatica: Being hypocritical. Fear
of money and/or the future.
Slipped Disc: Indecisive. Feeling
totally unsupported by life.
Sprains: Not wanting to move in a
certain direction in life. Anger and
resistance.
Stiffness: Rigid, stiff thinking.
Weakness: A need for mental
rest.

This case study illustrates the use of Epsom salt baths, rolling for release work, breathing practice, and acupuncture as techniques used effectively for releasing tension held within the body. Other methods include acupressure, pressure release work, tapping (or Emotional Freedom Techniques—EFT), and the practice of forgiveness. Tapping borrows principles from the ancient practice of acupuncture and combines them with contemporary psychology. Declaring your intentions while stimulating acupuncture points has been found to have distinct results, as confirmed by brain MRIs.[21] Forgiveness, long known as a virtue, is also seen as having distinct health benefits. It lowers blood pressure, increases the immune system, improves mood, and reduces overall stress.[22]

Emotions and thoughts are neither good nor bad. It is when they aren't paid attention to that they can become problematic. Additionally, **the actions you do take need to be ones that support your mission and are in congruence with your values.** Although this sounds obvious, it isn't unusual to do something contrary to our goal. For example, eating to fill an emotional void, shopping for comfort, and drinking to fit into a social group are all ways we use certain actions for an objective that meets a short-term goal that most likely isn't consistent with our long-term vision. When we detour like this, it can be helpful at revealing where our emotions are and what needs are not being met. Some of the most common attempts made in this way are for comfort, reassurance, excitement, diversion, anxiety, boredom, or depression. Getting

21 American Psychological Association, Review of General Psychology, December 2012: 16(4); 364-380.

22 Fred Luskin, *Forgive for Good: A Proven Prescription for Health and Happiness* (HarperCollins, 2002).

to the base of the emotion allows you to choose a more effective method to meet the need.

Remember in chapter 1 we saw that the heart has a measurable electromagnetic field? Emotions experienced from the heart will have a greater impact on your life than any thoughts you can generate. Combining thought with heartfelt emotion has the greatest impact, as you will see from this example with Linda as she pursued her life purpose.

Linda wanted more than anything to start a business. She had done all her homework, written the plans, checked off the lists, knew her market, and yet, nothing was happening. She couldn't figure out what was wrong. She came to me as a last resort.

When I talked with her, it was obvious she'd put full thought into every step. All the details regarding her business plan were in place and sound. Her passion was clothes and design, and she could tell me how she'd been sewing clothes proficiently since she was young, providing them to family and friends. But as she talked about her passion there was no spark. No light brightened her eyes and animated her. Something was definitely missing.

We began by clarifying her values, and she articulated her life purpose as creating beauty in a tangible way, with her mission as using her skills to help others feel more beautiful. Because Linda was such a visual and tactile person, I asked her to create a mood board representing her purpose and mission to help her develop her vision as well as feel emotion around her work.

As she combined fabrics and various media into a true work of art, Linda herself transformed. She continued working on the task of making her lists, but she had a new energy as she did, and she felt more creative as she approached the contacts necessary to help her with her dream. Her ideas became sharper and the plans more streamlined, giving her more time to create a clothing line she wanted to feature in her new store.

She paid attention to the tasks at hand while simultaneously enjoying the creativity that had fed her dream from the beginning. This action allowed her to freely demonstrate her enthusiasm for her ideas and business. Support quickly followed, and within six months Linda had her store.

The mood board is now framed in Linda's office as a reminder to continue creating your dreams while working your plans.

It is through combining the rational tasks and thought processes with the passion of the emotions and heart energy that the most effective progress is made. When you do this, you are harnessing all the energies within your body and putting them to work for you as you live your purpose.

The exercises below work on rational thoughts connecting to patterns in your life.

EXERCISE FOUR
MIND

1. Make a list of your favorite books, authors, songs, and places. Is there a theme that connects them?

2. Pay attention to random songs or phrases that occur to you. Write them down. What are the lyrics, and is there a pertinent message for you within them?

SPIRIT OR SUBCONSCIOUS

The subconscious is the puppet master overseeing all input and communication. The intuitive mind communicates through metaphors and symbols—images and messages that stir something within us from which we then identify further knowledge.

Messages from your subconscious are very personalized in the way you can best hear them; they are tailored to your idiosyncratic code of reception. This symbology is a result of you assigning meaning to signs and actions from your frame of reference, serving as a further mirror and signpost for contemplation and direction of purpose in your life.

Our distinctive fingerprint of understanding means we each have a unique equation of interpretation and translation. If you are musically inclined, you may notice song lyrics having particular application to an issue you are ruminating over. If you are extremely visual, you may notice recurring images at different times that trigger the same awareness.

Pay attention to the patterns that form, without giving them too much meaning initially. Have fun noticing how things happen for you in your life. Then, consider if that pattern has occurred in the past. To assign meaning to it for you now, reflect on what relevance it has to your daily life. Because you are working with the subconscious, don't be too literal. Allow the images and thoughts to form until you grasp a pattern that makes rational sense to you. These coincidences, as we see them, are what Carl Jung termed as synchronicities—to describe two events that have no relationship but seem connected.[23]

---

23 Carl G. Jung, *Synchronicity: An Acausal Connecting Principle.* (Bollingen, Switzerland: Bollingen Foundation, 1952.)

EXERCISE FIVE
SPIRIT/SUBCONSCIOUS

Reflect on the past week, looking for signs of synchronicity. Was there a theme that appeared in the conversations you had? Did a keynote dominate your reading choices or social media access? Did any insights occur to you through your dreams?

Your confidence and innate intuition—the knowledge that comes from deep within—will continue to expand as you put the patterns of your subconscious together. Events in your life will fall into a design that makes sense. You will be able to pull out information from the metaphors and symbols on topics you need. People that play a role in the next step of your work will show up. This is the syndrome of synchronicity, and you will see evidence of it increasing once you start paying attention to those messages your subconscious is sending you. By tuning into patterns in your life, you can gain clarity to stumbling blocks that are preventing you from moving forward as well as define steps of your life mission as it evolves.

Tim is a great example. He was very comfortable working within his physical and rational capabilities and indicated a sense of responsibility to control his environment to match his expectations, but when I asked him to stretch his comfort level and explore what information his subconscious might have for him, he was politely but frankly skeptical. He admitted he had vivid dreams and would relate them to me. I clearly saw a connection between his daily activities and his nightly subconscious messages, so I had confidence Tim's imagination was already well exercised. He just hadn't been tuning into it.

In our work together, Tim had experienced a great deal of success putting plans and action to his ideas and dreams, so he was willing to trust me enough to do some exercises despite his disbelief. He agreed that he had been experiencing fortunate coincidences in his life that were helpful in forming his business relationships, particularly when they most aligned with his largest vision. This surprised him because he often hadn't articulated this purpose or vision to his colleagues.

For the purpose of his exercise, I asked him to maintain a notebook and record all such coincidences and to consider that they were, in fact, synchronicities. In Tim's notebook he was to record coincidences that occurred in both his dreams and during the day. I reminded him that the subconscious speaks in metaphors, and they are not always mind-shattering insights. Thinking about hummingbirds during the day and then having a dream that features a hummingbird is the subconscious continuing the pattern of thought through your brain from rational (daytime) to subconscious (night dreaming).

After keeping these occurrences for a week, he was amused by the frequency but commented that they didn't appear to have any significance. I reminded him that the first stage was to observe and that the second was to interpret. Tim had meditation and contemplation as part of his Daily Practice. His assignment was to reflect on the interpretation during his contemplation.

Within a month, Tim's attitude lightened. His language didn't indicate he felt responsible for everyone else's happiness and for the outcome of the world. Instead, he had enthusiasm as he continued his plans and a renewed level of energy to initiate the groundwork on some new dreams. He enjoyed the "game" of tracking the metaphors of synchronicity so much that he continued keeping a dream journal and used it daily in his morning contemplation.

ENVIRONMENT

Your physical surroundings are a reflection of both what is within you and what is happening in your life. If your house is mayhem, that can signal your thoughts or direction in life is askew as well. In contrast, if everything in your house is in such perfect order that not one thread of a pillow fringe is astray, that can indicate your need for control of all aspects of life is unrealistic.

Chaos at home really hindered my client Rob's ability to move forward with his life purpose. At the time, he was a school administrator, living his purpose of raising the power of education as a tool for freedom. He was well liked and had a satisfactory personal life, although he hadn't had a romantic partner in his life since he'd been divorced over 15 years earlier. Always a little overweight, he'd steadily gained weight since high school, and at age 55, he was officially obese with many health problems as a causal side effect. His interaction with his two grown daughters was limited to them taking care of him or spending time with him in some way related to food. His income was generous, yet he was oddly in debt, and his car was barely holding together. His friends appreciated his warmth, humor, and generosity and overlooked his perennial tardiness.

When Rob approached me to work with him on a retirement plan, he needed help physically, mentally, and spiritually, but we started with the practical. I asked if we could meet at his house.

He showed me in, and I hid my shock at a house that was just short of qualifying for a hoarding makeover. I asked him to take me to his favorite room, where we could talk and I could take notes. We went into a room that was so full of objects that we couldn't sit down before moving items. Clearly, the work was obvious to me but not to Rob. Every item symbolized something to Rob, making it difficult for him to discard. Disrespecting that would be hurtful and harmful, as well as counterproductive. So I asked what his most fervent wish was. He immediately responded that he wanted to be able to easily socialize with his daughters and their families and friends.

We formulated a plan as to how he would see that come together—where they could meet, what they would do—and then, step-by-step, we figured out what it would take to get from where he currently was to that vision. Once he saw it was possible, Rob had all the motivation in the world and started right in.

It took him three months to clear one section of his house for his girls, but when he did, that corner of the house was gorgeous. That accomplishment encouraged him to move to the kitchen area so that he could prepare food for them, and the process continued.

Rob's situation was extreme, and he had a large house. It took him over three years to finish his transformation, but by the end of those three years he was a different man. At the end of the first year, his house was noticeably cleaner, his finances were in order, and he was driving a different car. The second year, his friends commented that he was no longer late and began to include him in more events. The increased activity had an affect on Rob's total health, as he improved his overall health habits and shed his excess weight in the process. We could have started anywhere with Rob, but by starting with his environment, he was able to see immediate results that had a deeper impact to encourage him onwards.

Putting your physical house in order will do far more than clean up your environment—it will allow you to move forward with your purpose. Where is the disorder? Pay attention. Different areas in your house can represent areas of your life that need attention.[24]

EXERCISE SIX
ENVIRONMENT[25]

Give some thought to the rooms in your living space and what you currently use them for. For this exercise, you may find it useful to walk through your home with a notebook and record your impressions.

Reflect on each of the following areas, what state they are in, and how you are using the space. Use the following questions as thought starters and continue with your own ideas.

1. The entry: Does it welcome and prepare?

2. The living space or family room: Does it allow for fun, joy, quiet, and regeneration?

3. The kitchen and dining area: Is it set for creativity and nourishment, for sharing, and for collaboration?

4. Your bedroom: Is there room for rejuvenation and love?

5. Your bathroom: Is there room for sustenance, nurturing, and preparation?

---

24 Lauren Rosefeld and Melva Green, *Breathing Room: Open Your Heart by Decluttering Your Home* (New York: Simon & Schuster, 2014).

25 *Exercise inspired by Breathing Room: Open Your Heart by Decluttering Your Home*, Lauren Rosenfeld and Melva Green.

6. Office, study, or workspace: Is there room for inspiration and productivity?

7. Child's room or other bedrooms: Is there room for privacy, rest, renewal, growth, and change?

8. Storage: Is it a place for well-kept memories?

Now, consider what is your greatest wish from that living space. What can you do to clear and prepare it for that purpose?

Paying attention to clues and listening to the information contained within brings us back to our purpose. Creating and maintaining alignment requires frequent adjustments along the way. This isn't an indication that something is wrong—just that something can more optimally set you on your path forward or direct you on a more rewarding course. There will always be challenges along the way, but don't allow them to hold you back. When you release whatever is holding you back and are open to the full power of your potential, you can finally shift onward in life. The breakthrough you have available from the aftermath of the challenge far outweighs the difficulty!

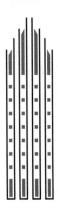

chapter eight

Visualizations and Meditations: Aid for Alignment

The soul attracts that which it secretly harbours; that which it loves, and also that which it fears; it reaches the height of its cherished aspirations; it falls to the level of its unchastened desires, and circumstances are the means by which the soul receives its own.

—JAMES ALLEN, *AS A MAN THINKETH*

As you've experienced from establishing your Daily Practice, Structure of Tactics, and Bundle of Exceptional Resources, finding your internal calm is an essential component of alignment. Having and maintaining an inner peace allows you to maintain alignment within, despite external circumstances. It doesn't matter where you fit centering into your day, whether it is in your Daily Practice or part of your Structure, but it is essential for total, lifelong alignment.

Just like the other tools and practices, the exercises in this chapter should adapt as your needs change so that they stay relevant to your life. Some of these visualizations and meditations are timeless. Others come from my own experience. From the time

I was a young girl, my mind would create images—sometimes to obliterate my fears, sometimes to protect my hopes, and often to send them off on a prayer. As I learned to read and discovered authors such as Shakti Gawain, Aldous Huxley, Buckminster Fuller, Ram Dass, and other mind/spirit pioneers, I was shocked by the synchronicity between what my imagination had spontaneously conceived and what these brilliant individuals had written. This continues to be true for me with current thought leaders.

The truth I derive from this is twofold: our consciousness has a commonality beyond everyday functioning that we can access through visualizations, and there is a collective consciousness. Once a thought exists, regardless of how original it may seem to the individual, that thought exists in some specific form.

We can access this information through our visualizations. As with any of your practices, the more personal you make your visualizations, the more powerful and pertinent to your life they will be. When you generate your own visions, you tap into the universal force of *creative* energy. Use these exercises to get your thoughts started, and then let your creative mind go!

You can apply these exercises in many ways. You can tap into the power of your brain for relaxation and stress release, meditation, or mental rehearsal and practice. You can use it to accomplish a goal such as developing confidence or to form and create a new plan. You can develop intuition, pray, access spiritual help, exercise the brain, heal the body and mind, and even enhance athletic performance. By relaxing and allowing your creative imagination to come through, you are able to access deep meaning and support in your life.

Before diving too quickly into the practices, it's important to distinguish between the terms. Generally, I have found the term *creative visualization* to apply to manifesting desires or goals such as attracting wealth, jobs, partners, and so on, while *visualization* is used generally for relaxation-oriented results. Don't get caught up by all the terms you see, though. Just use what makes sense to you and your life. When you want to evoke a future potential or bring some reality to a goal you've undertaken, it is helpful to know that a visualization technique may be just what you are looking for.

Although they are used interchangeably, meditation and visualization do not indicate the same activity. *Meditation*, in contrast to *visualization*, has no set mental image but is instead a clearing of thought, a freeing of space, and an invitation for thought to enter that open space. Both practices—visualization and meditation—have tremendous value and benefit and are not mutually exclusive.

The following exercises are suggestions and starters. Modify them for your best purpose and intention. Make them yours and get creative—have fun.

VISUALIZATIONS

Grounding Cord

This visualization is helpful for fostering a sense of peace and calm or groundedness. The grounding cord can also be used to energize yourself and prepare for your day.

Relax by going somewhere you can be alone for 10—20 minutes. Take several slow, deep breaths. Breathe naturally and feel yourself relax increasingly with each exhale. Continue breathing in an even rhythm until you feel this relaxed sensation.

Imagine that there is a long cord running from the base of your spine to the center of the earth. Regardless of where you move, this cord moves effortlessly with you, as if propelled by a powerful magnet.

Create the cord from a substance that has appeal to you—a twisted rope, a thick cord, soft feathers, a silken braid. Make sure there are no frays, tears, or obstructions in the cord. If you see any, imagine them washed away and recreate a perfect cord.

The end that is attached to your spine must be secure as well, with no frayed, loose ends.

You can continue this visualization by going into another, perhaps a meditation, or by coming into the present day by slowing opening your eyes when you are ready.

Mental Rehearsal—You're the Star!

Use this visualization for rehearsing a situation, defining a goal, for the manifestation of a dream, or any mental rehearsal. It is an excellent tool to use prior to public speaking, making a presentation, or giving someone an important message, to name a few.

Go to a quiet place where you will be undisturbed for at least 20 - 30 minutes. You want to allow ample time to fully develop detail for this visualization. Begin relaxing by sitting comfortably, closing your eyes, and breathing deeply. Imagine that with every inhale you are breathing fresh possibilities in and with every exhale, you are expelling all old, stale ideas, thoughts and actions. Continue until you feel very relaxed but still somewhat alert.

If you are feeling somewhat unfocused in general, create a grounding cord. Next, imagine in detail the event you are rehearsing or planning. Use all of your senses and put yourself in the center of the activity. You may even wish to see yourself on a stage, on a movie screen, or on a raised dais.

What do you *smell*? What do you *hear*? What do you *feel* under your feet? Do your fingers *touch* anything? What emotions are evoked—how do you feel? What are you wearing, and can you feel any sensations on your arms, legs, or anywhere else?

You are the star of this event, so make it the way you want it to be. If the first attempt isn't quite perfect, erase it with a giant eraser and recreate it. Every detail from your hairstyle, shoes, and clothes, to the flooring, sound, and scent are just as you imagine. What is the background noise? Whose voices, if any, do you hear? The more detail the better. The mind is forming neural pathways as you do this exercise, creating new potential as you visualize.

Once you have an image that fills you with almost uncontainable enthusiasm, think of a word, phrase, color, scent, or action that will be a reminder for you of this image and feeling. Come back to the present time when you are ready by slowly opening your eyes and writing down your reminder. It will be your key for returning to your perfect reality quickly.

This *Is* You

Often, you can benefit from rehearsing yourself at a higher level of achievement. This visualization is excellent for taking yourself there. It isn't for focusing on an *event* but rather on who *you* want to be in your full expression of yourself—the perfect, whole you. Once you have a precise image of yourself in the place you want to be, you can watch yourself in the future enjoying that reality. This is similar to the Mental Rehearsal, but in this visualization, *you* are the focus, not the event imagined.

Sit in a quiet place where you won't be disturbed for at least 20 minutes and up to an hour. Be sure you are relaxed and comfortable, breathing naturally through your nose with your eyes closed. As you inhale, imagine the air coming in through your nostrils is full of fresh ideas and potential. As you exhale, you are ridding yourself of all old patterns of behavior, thoughts, ideas and negativity. If thoughts of the day or details arise, just let them pass, and return to an easy breathing pattern. Continue until you are relaxed but still feel mentally alert.

Now, imagine yourself as you want to be in perfection. See yourself from head to toe, in detail, as you would like to be seen. Feel exactly what you want to feel like. Hear what sounds surround you when you are where you want to be. Is there a taste in your mouth? Are people around you? Who are they? What colors surround you? Where are you? See, feel, hear, and taste in detail.

Now, go through your perfect day. Begin by visualizing the bed you wake up in, in the ideal room in your chosen home, and in the area where you most want to live. Continue through your morning practices and routine, in detail. What are you wearing as you do them? Is there anyone else in your home? What sounds? What scents?

Visualize the day in full detail until you return to the bed for perfect sleep. As you slowly return to the current time and place, what details can you act on now? Are there steps you can take to making that reality one step closer? Write them down if that is useful and then begin making it real.

Clearing

Your brain and energy system of chakras hold images that were imprinted long ago, whether they currently benefit you or not. It is important to remove them once you no longer benefit from them. This visualization can easily clear old attachments and is excellent for a fresh start.

Begin by sitting in a chair where you won't be disturbed for 15–30 minutes and can fully relax without distractions. Slowly breathe, imagining that with every breath you are taking in clear, clean fresh air, and with every exhale you are expelling all thoughts, words, people, and actions that cause you any distress or discomfort. Whatever thoughts arise, let them pass without holding on and without judgment. Continue until you feel relaxed but not sleepy.

As you breathe in, visualize a channel of forceful energy, much like water, entering through the top of your head and continuing through the center core of your body through the bottom of your feet. This energy will circulate back in a cycle, and as it does, it washes away any and all attachments from your center and from your body, leaving only the healthiest parts of you. With each breath you take in, breathe in fresh energetic buoyancy. With every breath expelled, all attachments, debris, and heaviness within you fades away. Continue this breath cycle until only relaxation is felt.

Slowly return to the present when you are ready by opening your eyes.

MEDITATIONS

There are many books, courses, sites, apps, and other resources for meditation. Unfortunately, we waste a lot of time complicating the process. Meditation is as simple as spending some time every day to clear one's mind and invite a quiet space to enter. There is no *quality* of meditation. There is no judgment on whether a meditation is good or bad. The *process* itself is the objective and goal. As thoughts enter and distract you, just let them pass through. That, too, is part of the process. The following are just a few simplified ways to adopt meditation into your life.

Walking

If you think you are too busy to meditate because you are on the go all the time, this meditation will show you how easy it is to incorporate meditation into your current routine.

Go on a 20–30 minute walk, without music, dogs, or another companion for distraction, and use walking as the focus of mindfulness.

Begin by breathing, and ideally practice this meditation outside. Walk at a normal to slow—but not exaggeratedly slow—pace. Moving the body automatically puts the mind in a meditative state. Simply allow it. Become aware of all sensations. When your mind wanders, bring it back to the moment and the sensations in the body.

Breathe

Sit comfortably where you won't be disturbed for 20–30 minutes. Use your breath as your focus. Breathing normally, follow your breath in with each inhale and observe it out as you exhale. It can be helpful to visualize your breath as you do this. Picture a feather floating up and down with each breath in and out, a bubble of air inflating and deflating with each breath in and out, or any other image that is meaningful to you. When your mind wanders, return to the breath.

Return slowly to the current day and time when done by resuming your normal breathing pattern and opening your eyes.

Mantra

If you're looking for a more traditional practice to define your routine, the mantra will appeal to you. It doesn't require any special props, but you will want to go somewhere you feel comfortable.

Sit where you won't be disturbed for 20–30 minutes. In this meditation, a sound, word, or phrase is used repetitively. The repetition serves to calm and clear the mind.

Mantras can be anything from traditional ones given to you during an initiation, to personally choosing a word or a sound. Some choices might be "om, one, peace" or chanting a phrase such as "sat, chit, ananda," which translates to "existence, consciousness, bliss."

Silently repeat the mantra, allowing it to calm you and empty your thoughts. When the mind wanders, return to the mantra.

Return slowly to the current day and time when done by resuming your normal breathing pattern and opening your eyes.

Open Eye

If you're ready for a further challenge or if you'd like to fit in meditation while you are working or in a public place, this one's for you. This meditation can easily be done while you're waiting in your car.

Sit comfortably where you won't be disturbed for 20–30 minutes. Using a visual object as a focal point, breathe slowly and relax, concentrating on that object. If you are in a private place, the visual object may be a candle, a statue, a flower, or other symbolic object. Eyes remain open, focused solely on the object. When the eyes or the mind wanders, return to the central focus.

After the time period you've allotted for your meditation, return slowly to the current day and time by resuming your normal breathing pattern.

Chakra[26]

Chakra meditations are particularly helpful when you are integrating your body's physical, mental, and emotional intelligences. A meditation focused on an individual chakra can be very valuable if you are looking for peace of mind regarding a specific issue that's bothering you. It doesn't matter if you know and understand the chakra system. You can use the body's intelligence through this meditation. The meditation below is a comprehensive overview of all the chakras for balancing and is excellent for an overall good start to any day.

Begin by sitting where you won't be disturbed for 15–30 minutes and can fully relax without distractions. Slowly breathe, imagining that with every breath you are taking in clear, clean, fresh air and that with every exhale, you are expelling old trapped air and debris.

With the next breath in, imagine your incoming breath coming in from the very top of your head and scrubbing effervescent circles of cleansing energy as it moves from the top of your head through the core of your body to the bottom of your feet. Move slowly with this effervescent breath, taking time to pause at your forehead, scrubbing in circles, and then progressing to your throat, your heart, your solar plexus, your sacrum, and on to your tailbone. Breathe in a rhythm that is comfortable for you while breathing in clear effervescence and breathing out debris.

After clearing your core, take in a deep breath, carrying a clear effervescence through all chakras—through your legs and circling back up into the base of your spine, your sacrum, your

---

26 The chakras are our body's subtle energy system. For a complete explanation on the chakra system and resources, refer to the Resource section and the chart on page 150.

solar plexus, and your heart, and then move that air into your arms and out to the very tips of all fingers, bringing it back around and up into your throat, your forehead, and out the crown of your head. Continue this pattern until you have a very clear sense that there is no "debris" leaving your body.

The next clear breath in, add color as you travel through the chakras. As you go through the crown of your head, visualize violet light radiating and spinning. Let that continue as you move to your forehead and see indigo light radiating. You may experience the two colors beginning to merge. Allow whatever image or sensation is there and continue on to your throat. Add blue to your throat. Then move to your heart and expand your heart chakra with green. Move to your solar plexus and fill it with yellow. Proceed to your sacrum and infuse it with orange and finally to the tailbone, where you will add red.

Keep all your chakras radiating with healthy, vibrant color. When you are ready to return to the present time, resume your normal breathing pattern and slowly open your eyes.

CHAKRA CENTERS

Sahasrara

Ajna

Vishuddha

Anahata

Manipura

Svadhisthana

Muladhara

7th: The Crown
Sahasrara, above the crown. Higher Consciousness, Enlightenment, Inspiration. The Head Center, the thousand petaled lotus. Corresponds to the Universal Self –The Divine Reality, the color violet, and the Power of Consciousness.

6th: The Third Eye
Anja, between eyebrows. Intuition, Insight, Psychic Awareness, ESP. The Center of Command. Relates to the mind and the color blue, the individual Self, the power of inner perception, and Insight beyond the five senses.

5th: The Throat
Vishuddha, throat area. Creativity, Speech, Individual Needs and Will. The Very Pure. Relates to Ether and the color blue; the respiratory system, to higher intelligence, the Power of Communication.

4th: The Heart
Anahata, middle of chest. Love, Forgiveness, Compassion, Self-Esteem. The Center of Unstuck Sounds of the subtle body. Relates to the Air element and the color green; governs the circulatory system, the individualized soul, the emotion of Love.

3rd: The Navel
Manipua, solar plexus. Desire, Vitality, Inner Strength, Self Control. City of Gems. Corresponds to the element Fire and the color yellow; governs the digestive system, the ego impulse, the emotion Anger.

2nd: The Sacral
Svvadhisthana, above genitals. Relationships, Sexuality, Intimacy. Adobe of Kundalini. Relates to the Water element and the color orange; governs the sex instinct, the uro-genital systems, the emotion Desire.

1st: The Root
Muladhara, below genitals. Survival, Security, Primal energy. The Root Center. Relates to the Earth element and the color red; governs all elimination, the survival instinct, the emotion Fear.

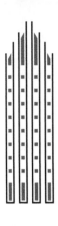

c h a p t e r   n i n e

Integration: Putting It All Together

Love is the affinity which links and draws together the elements of the world...Love, in fact, is the agent of universal synthesis...[It] is a sacred reserve of energy; it is like the blood of spiritual evolution.

—TEILHARD DE CHARDIN

As you've progressed through this book, you've done a lot of work organizing all the components of your life and yourself to go forward and live your life fully in the manner you envision it. Now what? How do you synthesize it?

INTEGRATE

Until you fully integrate something, it is not really yours. Your Personal Template, Daily Practice, Structure of Tactics, and Bundle of Exceptional Resources are just projects you've undertaken until you fully integrate them. Remembering the *why* of your initial incentive will keep you inspired. When your actions become a normal part of your day and your life, you have made them yours. Your brain has then assimilated the learning by creating new ways of thinking and being. Through neuroplasticity,[27] the new information has been incorporated into your physiology and is now a part of you.

It is through integrating knowledge that you solidify the learning and maintain alignment. As you do this, you are able to stay on track in living your purpose with dedication.

EXERCISE ONE
BOOK OF ME CHECK-IN

Take a look at the workbook you've created throughout this project.

- Does it fully respond to all the questions you have on your current journey? If not, write down what is missing. What do you need to do to find those missing pieces?

- Peruse your workbook. Does it represent you visually in a gratifying way? Make any modifications you would like now.

HAVE INTEGRITY

Similar to how you carefully defined your values in chapter 2, living your life in integrity requires you to be deliberate and consistent in how you think, speak, and act. When you live with integrity and fully integrate all three cornerstones of Body, Mind, and Spirit into your days, you will open the doors to living a life in

---

27 Sharon Begley, *Train Your Mind, Change Your Brain: How a New Science Reveals Our Extraordinary Potential to Transform Ourselves* (Ballantine, 2007).

alignment with your purpose and fully become part of something greater than yourself.

Integrity is directly reflected in the words we choose; honesty is often measured by the words we speak. Therefore, speak ever so carefully because words have tremendous power both to yourself and to your listener. Your choice of vocabulary expresses and reveals you uniquely—choose to use this power deliberately for your best outcome. For example, it is far more motivating to use words like "want to" and "get to" rather than "should," "need," or "must." Language forms mental images when we hear and use it. This imaging can have a powerful effect on your mission.

If Betty says, "I should use my organizing skills to work with homeless agencies," this sounds like her task belongs on a to-do list. Contrast that statement with, "When I use my skills at connecting people with practical tasks and deadlines, I am able to organize the delivery of leftover restaurant meals to homeless people that would be thrown away."

When Betty states what she thinks she should do, it sounds like a random thought. When she expresses it with personalized vocabulary, it sounds like she is committed to living her life in a certain way. If her words convey that message to us, consider how they feel to her as she says them. It's this empowering and motivating language that will help you live with integrity—if you follow through. Having positive, powerful thoughts and speaking about them will not be enough. You have to follow through with specific actions, feeling the impact of your assured result as you go. All three parts—thinking, speaking, acting—must be present to progress forward.

Remember to take command of your progress and change your language going forward. Monitor the words you use. It is one more way you are taking control of your life. By consciously choosing powerful words, you direct your actions and take control of your emotions.

INTEGRAL—MAKE IT NORMAL

When you are living your purpose, it is often with the result of making the world a better place, affecting change in some way. Doing your Daily Practice and all the steps you've established to maintain alignment will increase your comfort level and confidence to live your purpose daily. Knowing what you want to do in life and then hiding doesn't accomplish your goal. You need to make it an intrinsic part of your life going forward. Then it becomes normal.

We are all here to live our purpose. Whether we fulfill it or not remains to be seen. We aren't more spiritual than anyone else who isn't doing a morning practice or a Structure of Tactics. Choose whatever actions best support your ultimate objective, then go forward and live your life and just *make it normal.*

As you become more comfortable with the assimilation of new knowledge and practices, your capacity for additional information will increase simultaneously. To keep yourself on track for alignment, here are some reminders:

- Make yourself a priority because you value your purpose.

- Prioritize your activities to support your highest objective.

You know what is important to you. You live by a creed. You know your values, your purpose, your mission, your vision, and what it takes to stay in alignment to live that full-spectrum life. So prioritize your activities. Say no to whatever doesn't support your best life.

As you go through your day and see all the choices in front of you, you begin to see a common pattern and truth underneath all parts of your life. Nothing has to be very complicated or difficult, and it is easy to see connections in life. You can exercise your full creativity to make the most powerful choice for *your* needs. The creativity you put into presentation, detail, words, and effort will be uniquely you.

EXERCISE TWO
ALIGNED YOU

It can be useful to formalize the completion of your thoughtful contemplation and work. Set aside time to launch the new version of yourself. Consider the ideas below as possibilities, or come up with an alternative.

1. Go on a retreat: Either find an existing retreat or create one. This can be at a destination, or you can set aside a specific regime at home. If you structure a self-retreat, specifically designate times and activities, even if they are for "quiet time."

2. Day of silence: This can be done at home or while away—a day of silence in nature is ideal. Write in your journal or just contemplate.

3. Plan a reward or celebration: Whatever is meaningful to you will work best. Options include throwing a party, making a symbolic purchase, deciding to take a course, and undertaking a long-delayed dream, to name a few.

4. Ritual and ceremony: Create and enact a ritual honoring parts of you that no longer have a place in your life. Put the old you to rest and celebrate the life of the new you.

Rituals are powerful ways to mark a transition. The important elements are to mark the ending of the old you and honor the emerging you with a ceremony. For example, go to a place that has special meaning for you, such as your office or a favorite beach or nature area, light a candle if appropriate, and play music that represents you. Choose an image of the former you. Delete or burn it while remembering all the wonderful parts of your life that brought you to the current moment and made you who you are today.

Reflect on your future and next steps. What are your hopes? Select a symbol, words, or motto that represents the new beginning. Capture this in some way—write it down, photograph it, or draw it, to name a few possibilities. Choose an aspect from this exercise that you will place somewhere prominently to remind you—perhaps in your bathroom, on your desk, or in your car.

It is up to us to take who we are, use all that we can, and bring our unique gifts to the world. Full-spectrum living is the integration between values and purpose, the alignment between body, mind, and spirit, and the equilibrium between your personal and external world. What is your choice? Choose it and become it. It's not that complicated—and you have the tools to do it!

Resources

The following sources will give you further perspectives on the ideas introduced in this book. If you discover that you enjoy a book that is listed, do investigate other titles by that author. I've limited this list to correspond with the book content, but the authors shown have written other works of interest. I encourage you to build your personal list of resources in your workbook, annotating items of most significance to you. If you have questions about any of the practices, modalities or resources, and for even more templates, please contact me at www.JanLBowen.com.

GOAL SETTING

Allen, David. *Getting Things Done: The Art of Stress-Free Productivity.* New York: Penguin, 2015.

Covey, Stephen. *First Things First.* New York: Free Press, 1994.

TEMPLATE COMPONENTS

Writing:

Cameron, Julia. *The Artist's Way: A Spiritual Path to Higher Creativity.* New York: Tarcher/Penguin, 2002.

First of author's creativity series. Highly recommend all.

Yoga:

Chen, Christine. *Happy-Go-Yoga: Simple Poses to Relieve Pain, Reduce Stress, and Add Joy.* New York: Grand Central Life & Style, 2015.

Forbes, Bo. *Yoga For Emotional Balance: Simple Practices to Help Relieve Anxiety and Depression.* Boston: Shambhala, 2011.

Pilates:

www.balancedbody.com

Brooke, Siler. *The Pilates Body.* Portland: Broadway Books, 2000.

Breathing:

Farhi, Donna. *The Breathing Book.* Washington: Owl Books, 1996.

Laynee Restorative Breathing Method™:
www.restoringbreathing.com

Acupressure:

Gach, Ph.D., Michael Reed. *Acupressure for Emotional Healing: A Self-Care Guide for Trauma, Stress, & Common Emotional Imbalances.* New York: Bantam, 2004.

Creativity:

Pressfield, Steven and Shawn Coyne. *The War of Art: Break Through the Blocks and Win Your Inner Creative Battles.* Black Irish Entertainment, LLC, 2012.

Tharp, Twyla and Mark Reiter. *The Creative Habit: Learn It and Use It for Life.* New York: Simon and Schuster, 2006.

Gratitude:

Arrien, Angeles. *Living in Gratitude: A Journey That Will Change Your Life*, Boulder: Sounds True, 2013.

Lesowitz, Nina and Mary Beth Sammons. *Living Life as a Thank You: The Transformative Power of Daily Gratitude*. Poulsbo: Viva, 2009.

Emotional Freedom Technique (EFT):

Feinstein, David, Donna Eilen, and Gary Criag. *The Healing Power of EFT and Energy Psychology: Tap into Your Body's Energy to Change Your Life for the Better.* London: Piatkus Paperback, 2006.

Prayer:

Merton, Thomas. *A Book of Hours*. South Bend: Sorin Publishing, 2007.

Williamson, Marianne. *Illuminata*. New York: Riverhead Books, 1994.

> *Although she has written many other more recent books, this volume remains one of my favorites.*

Prayer:

Suzuki, Wndy. *Healhty Brain, Happy Life*. New York: Dey Street Books, 2015.

ASTROLOGY

Arroyo, Stephen. *Astrology, Psychology & the Four Elements: An Energy Approach to Astrology & Its Use in the Counseling Arts.* Sebastopol, CA: CRCS Publications, 1978.

Arroyo, Stephen. *Chart Interpretation Handbook Guidelines for Understanding the Essentials of the Birth Chart.* Sebastopol, CA: CRCS Publications, 1989.

Bloch, Douglas, and Demetra George. *Astrology for Yourself: A Workbook for Personal Transformation, How to Understand and Interpret Your Own Birth Chart.* Lake Worth, FL: Ibis Press, 2006.

NUMEROLOGY

Millman, Dan. *The Life You Were Born to Live: A Guide To Finding Your Life Purpose.* Tiburon: New World Library, 1993.

TAROT

Arrien, Angeles. *The Tarot Handbook: Practical Applications of Ancient Visual Symbols.* New York: Penguin, 1997.

Greer, Mary K. *Tarot for Your Self: A Workbook for Personal Transformation.* Wayne, NJ: Career Press, 2002.

Quinn, Paul. *Tarot for Life: Reading the Cards for Everyday Guidance and Growth.* Illinois: Theosophical Publishing House, 2009.

ENVIRONMENT

Kingston, Karen. *Clear Your Clutter with Feng Shui.* New York: Broadway Books: 1999.

> *A clear-cut explanation of feng shui and how to make a practical difference with it in your life.*

Rosefeld, Lauren, and Melva Green, *Breathing Room: Open Your Heart by Decluttering Your Home* New York: Simon & Schuster, 2014.

MINDFULNESS, MEDITATION, & VISUALIZATION

Bays, Jan Chozen. *Mindfulness on the Go.* Boston: Shambhala, 2014.

Chodron, Pema. *Meditation: How to Meditate: A Practical Guide to Making Friends with Your Mind.* Boulder: Sounds True, 2013.

Guide to traditional Buddhist meditation.

Dass, Ram. *Polishing the Mirror: How to Live From Your Spiritual Heart.* Boulder: Sounds True, 2014.

Gawain, Shakti. *Creative Visualization* and *Living in the Light.* New World Library, 1987.

Classics on visualization practice and techniques.

Kornfield, Jack. *Meditation for Beginners.* Boulder: Sounds True, 2008.

Simple step-by-step instructions on how to meditate.

Transcendental Meditation: www.tm.org

MIND/BODY CONNECTION: THE BODY'S INTELLIGENCE

Childre, Doc and Howard Martin. *The Heartmath Solution: The Institute of HeartMath's Revolutionary Program for Engaging the Power of the Heart's Intelligence.* San Francisco: HarperOne, 2000.

Myers, Thomas W. *Anatomy Trains Myofascial Meridians for Manual & Movement Therapists* London: Churchill Livingstone, Third Edition 2014.

Northrup, Christiane. *Goddesses Never Age: The Secret Prescription for Radiance, Vitality, and Well-Being*. California: Hay House, Inc., 2015.

Pert, Candace E. *Molecules of Emotion: The Science Behind Mind-Body Medicine,* New York: Scribner, 1997.

Ross, Julia. *The Mood Cure: The 4-Step Program to Take Charge of Your Emotions Today.* New York: Penguin, 2002.

An overview of how nutrition affects all aspect of functioning and presents solutions through nutrition.

Segal, Inna. *The Secret Language of Your Body: The Essential Guide to Health and Wellness*. New York: Simon & Schuster, 2010.

Viachonis, Vicky. *The Body Doesn't Lie: A 3-Step Program to End Chronic Pain and Become Positively Radiant*. New York: Harper One, 2014.

CHAKRAS

Forbes, Bo. "What's Up With the Chakras?" June 28, 2014. http://boforbes.com/yoga-practice-lab/blog/whats-chakras/

Judith, Anodea. *Wheels of Life: A User's Guide to the Chakra System*. Woodbury: Llewellyn Publications, 1999.
Classic text on comprehensive overview of chakras.

Tuttle, Carol. *Chakra 7*, MindValley, 2012.
A complete course with exercises for the chakras.

INSPIRATION

Brown, Brené. *Daring Greatly: How the Courage to Be Vulnerable Transforms the Way We Live, Love, Parent and Lead.* New York: Penguin, 2012.

Larkin, Geri. *Close to the Ground: Reflections on the Seven Factors of Enlightenment.* Berkeley: Rodmell Press, 2013.

Oliver, Mary. *Long Life: Essays and Other Writings.* Boston: DeCapo Press, 2005.

TED talks: https://www.ted.com/talks
  TED is a nonprofit dedicated to Ideas Worth Spreading. Look through the categories and find some that inspire you.

Whyte, David. *Everything is Waiting For You.* Ireland: Many Rivers Press, 2003.

THE POWER OF THOUGHT

Allen, James. *As A Man Thinketh.* free domain, original 1903.

Cousins, Norman. *The Healing Heart.* New York: Avon Books, 1984.
  One of the original works on the power of attitude and its effect on the body, and in this case, on healing.

Hicks, Esther and Jerry. *Manifest Your Desires: 365 Ways to Make Your Dream a Reality.* Berkeley: Hay House, 2008.

Hill, Napoleon. *Think and Grow Rich.* Los Angeles: Tarcher/Penguin Publishing, rev. 2005.

NEUROLINGUISTIC PROGRAMMING (NLP)

Dilts, Robert. *Sleight of Mouth: The Magic of Conversational Belief Change.* Capitola: Meta-Books, 1999.

Grinder, John and Richard Bandler. *The Structure of Magic, vol. I and II.* Mountain View: Science and Behavior Books, rev. 2005.

> Volume 1: A Book about Language and Therapy

> Volume 2: A Book about Communication and Change

NEUROPLASTICITY

Begley, Sharon. *Train your Mind, Change your Brain: How a New Science Reveals Our Extraordinary Potential to Transform Ourselves,* Ballantine, 2007.

Doidge, M.D., Norman. *The Brain That Changes Itself: Stories of Personal Triumph From the Frontiers of Brain Science.* New York: Penguin. 2007.

Hanson, Rick. *Buddha's Brain: The Practical Neuroscience of Happiness, Love, and Wisdom.* Oakland: New Harbinger Publications, 2009.

INTEGRATED LEADERSHIP

Barrett, Richard. *The Values-Driven Organization: Unleashing Human Potential for Performance and Profit.* New York: Routledge, 2014.

Seale, Alan. *Create A World That Works: Tools for Personal & Global Transformation,* San Francisco: Red Wheel, 2011.

Seale, Alan. *Intuitive Living: A Sacred Path,* San Francisco: Red Wheel, 2001.

GENERAL

Dyer, Wayne W. *Your Sacred Self: Making the Decision to be Free.* New York: Harper. 1995.

Jaworski, Joseph. *Synchronicity: The Inner Path of Leadership.* San Fransisco: Berrett-Loehler Publishers, 2011.

Peat, F. David. *Synchronicity: The Bridge Between Matter and Mind.* New York: Bantam, 1989.

Printed in the USA
CPSIA information can be obtained
at www.ICGtesting.com
JSHW012052140824
68134JS00035B/3401